THOMAS
CHRISTIANSON

THE UNREASONABLE
JESUS

BECOMING THE PERSON
HE MADE YOU TO BE

JESUS-CENTERED **J.**

Credits
Chief Creative Officer: Joani Schultz
Senior Editor: Mikal Keefer
Assistant Editor: Lyndsay Gerwing
Art Director: Jeff Storm
Designer & Production Artist: Darrin Stoll

Scripture quotations are taken from the *Holy Bible,* New Living Translation, copyright ©1996, 2004, 2007, 2013, 2015 by Tyndale House Foundation. Used by permission of Tyndale House Publishers, Inc., Carol Stream, Illinois 60188. All rights reserved.

Library of Congress Cataloging-in-Publication Data
Names: Christianson, Thomas, 1978- author.
Title: The unreasonable Jesus : becoming the person He made you to be / Thomas Christianson.
Description: First American Paperback [edition] . | Loveland, CO : Group Publishing, Inc., 2018. | Includes bibliographical references. | Identifiers: LCCN 2017032279 (print) | LCCN 2017046345 (ebook) | ISBN 9781470748647 (ePub) | ISBN 9781470748654 (Audio book) | ISBN 9781470748630 (first american pbk.)
Subjects: LCSH: Sermon on the mount.
Classification: LCC BT380.3 (ebook) | LCC BT380.3 .C47 2018 (print) | DDC 226.9/06--dc23
LC record available at https://lccn.loc.gov/2017032279

ISBN: 978-1-4707-4863-0
Printed in the U.S.A.
10 9 8 7 6 5 4 3 2 1   27 26 25 24 23 22 21 20 19 18

INTRODUCTION

Just about everybody likes Jesus.

My Jewish friends say he's a great teacher. My Muslim buddies read about Jesus in the Quran and esteem him highly as a prophet. A quote attributed to the famous Hindu believer Gandhi says, "I like your Christ; I do not like your Christians."[1]

Politicians often portray themselves as Jesus' BFF to win votes. A wide range of Christian groups and denominations point to themselves as the people who *really* understand Jesus.

Jesus shows up in movies. You'll find him on jewelry, bumper stickers, and tattoos. And I've long ago quit counting all the songs written to, for, and about Jesus.

That's all great. I'm a big fan of Jesus.

But I have a question: Would he be as popular if we actually read what he says? *All* the stuff he says?

For example:

"Cut off your hand and gouge out your eye if they cause you to sin."

"Eat my flesh and drink my blood."

"Being angry and insulting someone is as bad as committing murder."

"Never seek revenge."

"Love your enemy."

Those aren't the quotes that end up on bumper stickers because…well, they're completely unreasonable. Were someone other than Jesus to say those things to me, I'd nod slowly while backing out of the room.

But Jesus says them…and appears to mean them…and still we claim him for our own.

So how does he pull it off?

I think, quite simply, we choose to ignore Jesus when he says anything too outrageous or unreasonable. We treat him like a crazy, rich uncle, smiling at his insanity because we don't want to get cut out of the will.

After all, we Christians believe it's through Jesus that we gain eternal life. With that kind of payoff, I can look the other way when he's being a little nutty.

And yet…

What if ignoring the unreasonable stuff means we're missing out on truly knowing Jesus, having a more authentic friendship with him?

What if "Unreasonable Jesus" is just as real as "Compassionate Jesus" and "Suffering Savior Jesus" and "Sweet Baby in the Manger Jesus"?

What if those "unreasonable" comments lead us to a healthier life—emotionally, spiritually, and relationally?

---

1   Gandhi actually said, "First, I would suggest that all of you Christians…must begin to live more like Jesus Christ." E. Stanley Jones, *Mahatma Gandhi: An Interpretation* (New York: Abingdon-Cokesbury Press,1948), 51.

What if Jesus asks us to grapple with those hard truths because that's one place we'll experience the transformation he's wanting to accomplish in us?

The Sermon on the Mount is one of the best places to meet Unreasonable Jesus and see him catch everybody—religious leaders and average people alike—completely off guard.

You've heard the sermon and read it in the Bible. But to get the full impact of what Jesus says, it helps to be mindful of where Jesus was and who was around him. Let me paint that picture for you.

It's at the front end of Jesus' ministry, and his popularity is skyrocketing. He's been teaching in area synagogues, traveling around the region of Galilee, and the word's out: If you're diseased, paralyzed, or demon-possessed, and you can make it to Jesus, he'll heal you. No charge.

So life's become a circus. Crowds have arrived, mobs of people either hoping for healing or eager to see the show. People elbow one another to get close to Jesus, the better to see and hear him or, hopefully, get a healing touch.

And as "Jesus fever" ramps up, Jesus hikes up a mountainside—the closest thing to picking up a microphone that existed at the time—finds a good place to sit down, and begins to talk.

The crowd listens intently, eager to hear what he has to say, sure they won't be bored. And they're not wrong, because Jesus says things they've never heard from a rabbi before. From *anyone* before, ever.

Those are the words we're going to explore together, considering what Jesus' words tell us about him…and about ourselves.

And we'll ask a dangerous question: *What if we actually do what he tells us to do?* Where do we start? How will it look? What will happen?

I'll share stories and practical insights from my journey of attempting to take Jesus' sermon seriously. And I'm inviting you to join Jesus in crafting new stories in your life as the two of you move along your journey together.

Jesus' words give us glimpses of the people he's calling us to become. And they show us how far we are from fully arriving.

But that's okay. We're on our way…together.

You and me.

Taking steps of faith.

Letting Jesus transform our lives.

A quick note: Jesus' sermon includes the "Beatitudes," that list of "blessed ares" that has kept theologians busy for centuries. And one can argue that expecting anyone to be happy about suffering because someday she'll inherit the earth is unreasonable in the extreme.

But Unreasonable Jesus was just getting warmed up. The Beatitudes were just the opening notes of his symphony.

That's why we're diving in at Matthew 5:13, when Jesus pushes past his opening salvo to dig deeper into the topics he wants his audience to consider.

So strap in.

We're about to meet the Jesus who's often ignored: the Unreasonable Jesus.

Chapter 1
SALT AND LIGHT

*You are the salt of the earth. But what
good is salt if it has lost its flavor? Can you
make it salty again? It will be thrown out
and trampled underfoot as worthless.*

*You are the light of the world—like a city on a
hilltop that cannot be hidden. No one lights a
lamp and then puts it under a basket. Instead,
a lamp is placed on a stand, where it gives light
to everyone in the house. In the same way, let
your good deeds shine out for all to see, so that
everyone will praise your heavenly Father.*

—Matthew 5:13-16

The Roman Emperor Julian (332–363) was not a fan of Christianity.
He hoped to restore the glory of the ancient Roman religion, one in which
a multitude of deities was worshipped in the temples and shrines scattered
across Rome.

But Julian encountered a problem when trying to convince Roman citizens
to turn their backs on the recently authorized Christian faith: the power of love
in practice.

Here's how Julian said it: "[Christianity] has been specifically advanced
through the loving service rendered to strangers…[The Christians] care not
only for their own poor but for ours as well; while those who belong to us look
in vain for the help that we should render them."[1]

---

1   Stephen Neill, *A History of Christian Missions* (London, Penguin Books,1964),
     37-38.

In other words, how could a pagan religion hope to gain followers when Christianity set itself apart through compassion and generosity?

But that was then, and this is now.

Unfortunately, Christianity doesn't enjoy such a lofty reputation any longer.

A couple of years ago I was scuba diving in Bermuda. After I was put in a group with other divers, the conversation turned toward the inevitable question: What do you do for a living? When I responded that I was a pastor and professor, my new acquaintances' looks of surprise, confusion, and concern told me there would be no follow-up questions.

Perhaps you've had a similar response on an airplane or at a family reunion when the topic of faith came up.

In the book *unChristian*, David Kinnaman reports that the majority of young Americans view Christianity as judgmental, hypocritical, overly political, anti-homosexual, out of touch, and insensitive.

Kinnaman sums up his finding with this statement: "We [Christians] have become famous for what we oppose rather than who we are for."[2]

How did that happen? How did a church so generous and giving that even an emperor couldn't swing public opinion back to his preferred religion get to the point where we are today? How did the church's reputation get so bad that it shuts down conversations on a scuba-diving boat before those conversations even get started?

I believe Kinnaman put his finger on one reason: People expect us to use our faith as a way to point out all their faults and shortcomings. I imagine what went through the heads of the couple I was about to join under the sea[3] was something like this: "Better not let this guy know what I'm up to in my personal life; I'll never hear the end of it."

We (and by "we," I mean Christians) have tragically found a way to do exactly what Jesus asks his listeners *not* to do: Hide their light under a basket. Bottle up the saltiness of their influence.

In this case, I'd suggest we all too often hide the gospel of love, light, and hope under the basket of criticism and self-righteousness.[4]

You can't be salt and light without being actively engaged with the world around you, and the church is, by and large, not engaged in the broader culture. Perhaps that's because many Christians—at least Christians in America—believe they're at war with their culture.

Few Christians would say they've declared war in so many words, but consider the terms of engagement with culture. See if any have unintentionally wiggled their way into how you're living out your faith:

---

2   David Kinnaman, *unChristian* (Grand Rapids, Baker Books, 2007), 26.

3   Please tell me Sabastian from *The Little Mermaid* started singing in your head when you read that phrase. I need to not be the only one.

4   I promise this book isn't just me railing about Christians getting it wrong. I love my brothers and sisters in the body of Christ. This isn't about ME criticizing YOU or even THEM. It's about Jesus challenging US.

- We must be diligent about not being influenced by "outsiders" (that is, anyone not part of the Christian community). Especially suspect are sources of entertainment like Hollywood and Disney.

- We must publicly criticize (and perhaps protest or boycott) companies and celebrities when we don't approve of their behavior.

- We must fight in the arenas of politics, media, education, and law to ensure that our moral code is forced on everyone. Dialogue isn't a priority—winning is.

- We have an obligation to confront others when we believe they're living contrary to biblical ideals. It's our duty to continually occupy moral high ground and assert why our beliefs and values are superior to the beliefs and values of anyone who disagrees with us.

Meaning we become light hidden under a bushel. Salt locked inside salt shakers.

Compare those rules of cultural engagement with the ministry of Jesus, with how he went about engaging with the world.

Were Jesus to show up today, I suspect "Culture Warrior Christians" would almost certainly hate him. He'd spend time with ex-cons, hookers, junkies, and pretty much anybody who needed a message of hope rather than a message of condemnation.

And he'd refuse to let his message and ministry be co-opted by any political position. I say that because back when Jesus was delivering his sermon, it would have been easy and popular for him to denounce the occupying Roman government and army. Yet he didn't do it.

Instead, he commended the faith of a Roman Centurion. He told people to pay their taxes. When people wanted to declare him king and go to battle for him, he simply walked away.[5]

Jesus' purpose is bigger than fighting culture; he's interested in *redeeming* it. And that certainly strikes some of his followers as an unreasonable—perhaps even unwise—goal.

Jesus tells his listeners something that's as remarkable as it is unreasonable: They'll play a part in how he'll redeem their world.

"Redeeming" is something of a foreign concept to many of us. We live in a consumer-driven culture where if something's broken, we toss it and get a replacement.

But God isn't a consumer. He's a creator.

---

5   "Read my lips: Pay your taxes" wouldn't be an applause line then any more than it would be today. Fortunately, Jesus wasn't trying to win an election to become Messiah.

You've undoubtedly heard John 3:16 more than once: "For this is how God loved the world: He gave his one and only Son, so that everyone who believes in him will not perish but have eternal life."

That's why Jesus is sitting on a hillside delivering this sermon to a crowd. He's loving them, telling them truth. The entire reason God came to earth in the person of Jesus is for love.

God lovingly created this world and never stopped loving it—along with each person in it.

When something's broken, God looks for an opportunity to make it as good as new. That's what he's doing in our relationship with him through the sacrifice of Jesus. That's what he's doing when he gives us his Holy Spirit to heal the broken, hurting, corrupt areas of our lives.

And that's what he's doing when Jesus calls us to join him in healing the rest of the world, too. Which *will* happen, by the way. In the book of Revelation, God promises to make all things new again.[6]

In the meantime, Jesus hasn't deputized us to attack the people and culture around us. He *has* called us to influence both to turn toward the Creator and be part of a renewed future.

Do you see what's unreasonable here?

It's unreasonable to come up against a force that's pushing against what you believe and, rather than fight it, settle for influencing it through kindness and compassion. To engage in civil conversation instead of civil war.

To be salt and light.

But don't be mistaken: Both salt and light are powerful. Far more powerful, as our friend Julian discovered, than bullying and bombast.

Just as salt enhances the flavor of food, our influence can bring out some of the original flavor of this world: a world where death and decay were never supposed to have an impact.[7]

And just as even a dim light shining from a cabin calls to a person lost and wandering in the dark, we can draw people toward a place of peace and contentment.

Christian culture warriors believe our light is like a hazard light, designed to warn of danger and destruction. Yet Jesus doesn't use that image.

Jesus describes a light that attracts those who need a place of sanctuary. A light that provides a way to see that place of refuge clearly.

But, practically speaking, how do we live in such a way that we shine out a light that can shift culture? How can we be salt that gives those who taste us a hunger for Jesus? What's a reasonable response to Jesus' unreasonable expectation?

Let me suggest three culture-shifters you can live out today...

---

6   Revelation 21:5
7   Romans 8:21

Do good deeds.

If you want to help point any particular person (or group of people) toward a friendship with Jesus, I'd encourage you to find ways to serve them.

Lighting the way to Jesus requires that you have influence with people. That only comes in the context of a relationship, and building a relationship starts when you show people you value them. That may involve providing for a physical need, or it can be as easy as starting a conversation.

I was once out for a run in my local park when I saw a pavilion with a banner hung across the front that announced that the people meeting there were part of a local "Pagan Society."

I stopped running, walked over, and told them I noticed their banner and asked them about their group—who they were and what they were all about. Nobody wanted to talk to me.[8]

I'm assuming most of the pagan society's spur-of-the-moment interactions aren't positive. Eventually, I was pointed to the leader of the society. I sat down and had a conversation that started with me asking about their beliefs and then listening to what the leader had to say.

When she asked me what I believed, I was happy to share.

She told me they worship nature. I told her that I also love nature, and as a follower of Jesus, I believe nature is a gift to humanity from a God who loves us.

When I walked away from that brief encounter, the people in that group—all of whom had been listening in—knew that a Christian had just been respectful and friendly to their leader. My interaction was an opportunity to build a bridge instead of a wall.

If you aren't part of a faith community that provides opportunities to launch relationships and do good deeds in your community, I suggest you look into the Salvation Army or another organization that allows you to genuinely care for people through action.

Seriously. You may not be saved by doing good works, but you certainly shake salt liberally as you do them.

Shine—and explain why you're shining.

Feel free to share what you're doing on social media or other outlets, but also share the reason for those good deeds. Keep in mind the purpose for serving others is to direct praise to God, not yourself. To open up conversations, not collect accolades.

That can make selfies of you swinging a hammer or dropping off groceries tricky.

---

8   Literally the first time something like that ever happened to me. Aside from all four years of high school. And middle school before that. I'm going to stop talking now.

Remaining humble in the midst of putting others first is hard, so if sharing about it takes you to a place where you have a hard time doing it for the right reasons, share selectively. Or decide to keep it off social media altogether.

My point: According to Jesus, good deeds are meant to shine like a city on a hill, not a spotlight on ourselves.

I recently found myself in an unexpected job transition. When I shared about this sudden development on Facebook, numerous friends sent me messages of support and encouragement.

One of the most meaningful messages was from a co-worker I met during my days as a corporate employee, prior to my moving into full-time ministry.

His message explained that he was an atheist, something I was unaware of because we didn't have much opportunity to talk at our former place of employment. He said he liked my posts—while not subscribing to the theology in them—and that he admired people of faith.

I was so grateful to receive this message.

Our good deeds and life of faith can be inviting, like a campfire in the woods, or uninviting, like a flashlight in the eyes. My former colleague was telling me I'd lit a welcoming path toward Jesus, and that's something I'm always hoping to do.

Contribute to culture; don't just criticize it.

If you think a piece of art, a charity, or a politician is pointing away from God's Kingdom, then create something pointing toward it.

Anyone can criticize. If you want to make a difference in my life, do what Jesus did: *Show me something better*.

Jesus didn't focus on attacking the unhealthy religious and political practices of his day. He spent his time pointing toward something better.

Mother Teresa didn't exhaust herself railing against the caste system in Calcutta. Instead, she poured out her life offering care to people who were literally dying in the streets.

The reality is that culture and society aren't the enemy. They're necessary in life, and we won't shift culture by censoring music, television, film, painting, sculpture, government, education, or any other expression of culture and society. And I think we've proven we can't get away with replacing what exists with sub-par examples that just happen to be Christian.

But we *can* provide something better: artistically compelling alternatives with redemptive value.

I'd love for every follower of Jesus to explore being an artist. Writing, pottery, playing an instrument, photography, dancing, theater, poetry, storytelling, cake decorating, whatever—it all counts.

Why? Because we're all made in the image of a creative God. And the arts are how we can share our stories—and shine our lights—in a way culture willingly embraces.

God is artistically generous with our world—think beautiful sunsets and majestic mountains. He tells his story through creative means, and as his children, we're invited to follow his example.

When I realized Jesus was calling me to contribute rather than just critique, I reached out to others in my church community who engage in the art of writing. We meet regularly to encourage and challenge each other, pushing toward excellence so what we create will contribute beauty to our world.

You may be a woodworker, knitter, storyteller, baker, or maker of internet cat memes. Whatever your skill, gift, or passion, there's not only room but a *need* for you to utilize it. You need to do it for your own sake and for the sake of shining brightly and sprinkling salt in your community.

Jesus doesn't allow us the luxury of a bunker mentality, hiding out in a tight world of fellow believers.

He's calling us to be in this world *and* not of it,[9] which is the perfect spot for shining and saltiness…if we're willing to join him in engaging his world.

You up for it?

---

9   Taken from John 17:15-16. Often this verse is summarized as "in this world *but* not of it." I believe the word *and* is a better representation of the text.

▌▌ A Brief Pause

Shining. Being salty. They're both ways to have an impact on the wider world.

Take a few moments to consider these questions. Jot down your thoughts. Listen for what Jesus may be telling you about himself—and you.

What does this section of Jesus' sermon tell you about Jesus?

_____

_____

_____

What does your response to Jesus' expectation that you be shining and salty reveal about you?

_____

_____

_____

_____

How do you feel about the idea that you're creative? In what ways do you see yourself that way? And in what ways might your creativity point toward Jesus?

_____

_____

_____

_____

Chapter 2
THE LAW

Don't misunderstand why I have come. I did not come to abolish the law of Moses or the writings of the prophets. No, I came to accomplish their purpose. I tell you the truth, until heaven and earth disappear, not even the smallest detail of God's law will disappear until its purpose is achieved. So if you ignore the least commandment and teach others to do the same, you will be called the least in the Kingdom of Heaven. But anyone who obeys God's laws and teaches them will be called great in the Kingdom of Heaven.

But I warn you—unless your righteousness is better than the righteousness of the teachers of religious law and the Pharisees, you will never enter the Kingdom of Heaven!

—*Matthew 5:17-20*

The First Testament[1] of the Bible can be challenging to read.

I mean, seriously, who gets excited when reading Leviticus?[2] All those details about how to kill animals for sacrifice, what kind of facial hair priests

---

1   Also commonly known as the Old Testament. I use the term *First Testament* because when we call it "Old," it feels easier to ignore. "Ah, that's the old one. Throw it away, and use the new one instead."

2   Put your hand down—you're lying.

can sport, different ways to get defiled…You may have fallen asleep just reading that last sentence. Long lists of detailed instructions drone on for what feels like forever in several of the early books in the Bible.

And then there are other parts of the First Testament I'd rather ignore. All those places where people are dragged out to be stoned for various infractions.[3] God's demand that Israel exterminate different people groups.[4]

I'd much rather skip over all that and focus on the New Testament. Jesus never kills anybody or goes on and on about rules and regulations. He stays busy forgiving, healing, and accepting people, often without them even asking for it![5]

So why is it that instead of announcing that there's a new day dawning and we can ignore everything written before his arrival on earth, Jesus says he's not here to abolish the law? To me, Jesus and the First Testament often feel like opposites.

It feels unreasonable to hang on to the First Testament stuff and grab hold of Jesus' message at the same time, so how am I supposed to pull off that balancing act?

To address this question, we first need to take a look at how God views time. As in, the space-time continuum. No, I'm not about to go all science fiction on you.[6]

The writer of the book of Hebrews said, "Jesus Christ is the same yesterday, today, and forever" (Hebrews 13:8).

When we consider that passage alongside 2 Peter 3:8,[7] it seems that the writers of Scripture are telling us that God is nonlinear. In other words, there is no such thing as time in the realm of heaven.

I'll stop with the metaphysics now, but here's why it matters: When we're talking about why Jesus delivers his unreasonable expectation that we continue paying attention to the rules and regulations from the "bad old days," Jesus doesn't view the First Testament as "how God used to be."

Rather, those Scriptures describe the same God who came as the person of Jesus Christ. They describe the God who died on the cross. They describe the God who promises to make all things right again.[8]

For us, time is a progression. But for God, there's no progression; everything simply *is*. There's no change from angry God to nice God because

---

3   See Leviticus 20 and Deuteronomy 22 for multiple examples.

4   Deuteronomy 7:1-2

5   John 8:1-11: Jesus forgives the woman caught in the act of adultery without her even asking. // Mark 2:1-12: Jesus forgives and heals a paralyzed man apparently based on the faith of his friends. // Luke 8:40-56: A woman with a bleeding issue touches Jesus without asking permission and is healed.

6   I could totally do that, though. Any show/movie that starts with *Star*, I'm probably in on. *Trek, Wars, Gate*. Not *Search* though—that's a whole different enchilada.

7   "But you must not forget this one thing, dear friends: A day is like a thousand years to the Lord, and a thousand years is like a day."

8   Revelation 21:5

the same God currently extending you extraordinary grace is also currently ordering the slaughter of the Amalekites in 1 Samuel 15:3.

The loving God in whom you currently place your hope is, right now, ordering the stoning of murderers and idolaters.[9]

That's a brain stopper, right?

I struggle to embrace the grace-filled ministry of Jesus while also embracing some of what's in the First Testament. Maybe you do, too—lots of Christians do. But Jesus isn't giving us much of a choice here in his sermon.

I believe the life and ministry of Jesus is (and always has been) part of God's plan for this world. Everything God does in the First Testament is preparation for Jesus' arrival.

Think of it like this: One of the few specialty dinners I make is Kung Pao chicken.[10] When I decided to make this dish for the first time, I had to find a recipe, shop at multiple stores to buy ingredients, gather proper cooking utensils, and set aside enough time to make the meal.

I couldn't cook unless I first prepared.

If we want to understand what Jesus has come to accomplish, we need to understand the preparation undertaken in the 927 chapters between Genesis 3 (the fall of humanity) and the beginning of the New Testament.

In doing so, we see why Jesus embraces those writings instead of ignoring them or pushing them away. After all, what sort of cook would show up and say, "Throw out all the ingredients so I can get cooking"? It would make no sense.

If the First Testament sets the stage for Jesus' life and ministry, we'd be unwise to ignore it. View the First Testament through the following three filters and you'll see God's purpose and plan shining through all the rules and regulations. No wonder Jesus doesn't want his followers—including us—to skip past them.

God wants to bless, not harm.

When God chooses Abraham to become a great nation of people who receive a special status, God specifically says he does so because the entire world will benefit.[11]

Which means if Israel forgot its identity as a people set apart by God, all of humanity would lose its pathway to God's blessings.

So God was understandably severe about health practices, food regulations, civil requirements, and even waging war with other peoples. He's intent on protecting this nation tasked with being a bridge to God's blessing for the whole earth.

---

9   Leviticus 24:17; Deuteronomy 17:2-5
10   It's delicious. You should definitely email/tweet/message me for the recipe. I don't
     want to overstate this, but it's the greatest meal in the history of taste buds.
11   Genesis 12:1-3

It's like a doctor amputating a leg to save a life; it's a terrible option but better than the alternative.

God wants Israel to appreciate that they're different, so when he forbids wearing shirts made from two different materials, it's an object lesson—a reminder that his people aren't to intermarry with tribes who are unfaithful to the God of Israel.

God wants his people to remember they're chosen, called to live by his standards, not standards set by anyone else.

Even if some of these First Testament regulations no longer apply to you (such as how to compensate people gored by an ox[12]), you can still see the great care God puts into guiding and protecting his people.

The people he intends to use as the conduit for salvation, renewal, and restoration to the entire world.

Including you. And me.

I'm not a direct descendant of Abraham (in other words, I'm a Gentile, not a Jew), but I understand this sense of being called to be a vehicle of God's blessing to the world. That's absolutely the calling the church has inherited through the generosity of Jesus' salvation. And without seeing how it played out through Abraham and his descendants, I wouldn't understand the purpose and mission of the church today.

Jesus didn't come to abolish the law because the law was never about God micromanaging our behavior. It's always been about helping us understand our role as being conduits of God's blessing.

A personal example: I'm terrible with directions. I mean, utterly useless without a GPS device telling me what to do.

Fortunately, I married a woman who has an excellent sense of direction.

As a young husband, I'd doubt my wife when she told me where to turn en route to a destination. It only took me a few years too long to realize that I should probably listen to her rather than debate which way to turn.

My wife and I were in the same car. We were going to the same place. And she had the tools to get us there. How silly was it for me not to trust her when I wasn't sure what to do?

Likewise, Jesus is waaaaaaaaay smarter than I am (he sees all of human history, while I have trouble keeping track of my three kids at the mall), and he's for me rather than against me.[13] If Jesus tells me something is helpful, I should probably listen because when I listen to Jesus, things tend to go better.

I can either argue and debate or get moving in the right direction.

Those were the options available to the crowd listening to Jesus as he preached the Sermon on the Mount. The same options are available to us today. And we can learn a great deal by noticing how Israel responded to those options throughout the First Testament.

---

12 Exodus 21:28-30. No disrespect intended to anybody out there who owns an ox with a bad temper.

13 Romans 8:31

God's warnings are a reflection of his mercy.

I once had a professor announce on the first day of the class when our final paper was due. He told us that any paper turned in after that date would receive a zero.

Then he said, "Some of you will come to me the day before the paper's due, or the day it's due, and tell me you need more time, that you need a grace period. Here's the grace I'm giving you: I'm telling you 16 weeks before the paper's due that I will not accept it late."

More than a few students thought the professor was a huge jerk. I *loved* him. I knew exactly what I had to do to pass the course.

Through the prophets, God constantly reminds the Jewish people of their identity so they can remain faithful or make changes to avoid the consequences of terrible choices.

God doesn't warn his people about the consequences of disobeying him because he's mean. He warns them—warns *us*—because he's a loving Father. And Jesus clearly intends for us to hear those warnings and take them to heart.

God is intentional about teaching his people to love.

In *Desiring the Kingdom*, James K. A. Smith argues that our actions are influenced more by our hearts than our heads.[14]

In other words, we believe and desire before we pause to really think. Which is why, even though I'm fully aware carrots are healthier than potato chips, salty snacks are far likelier to end up in my shopping cart.

I crave chips. I desire chips. I *need* chips.

I'm well aware of the relative health benefits of chips versus carrots. What's needed to keep me on the straight and narrow isn't more information; it's heart transformation. It's valuing my health more than the crisp, salty snap of a fresh kettle chip as I gently lift it out of the bag and pop it in my mouth.

Unless I'm intentional as I make choices while at Whole Foods,[15] until I value my health more than the crunchy gratification of chips, I'll find myself in the snack aisle every time.

What I need is help reorienting my heart toward health. And, spiritually speaking, that's what the First Testament does for Jesus' followers. That's where we see what God values, what people like us value, and how choices play out.

God is all about teaching his people to know and love him, so he doesn't hide who he is. We see him in all his glory throughout the First Testament and how loving and obeying him leads to a healthy, happy life.

And how ignoring or disobeying him leads…elsewhere.

When we know the God whose story is told in the pages of the First Testament, it's easier to recognize the God we encounter in the New Testament, the God perched on a hillside delivering a sermon that changes everything.

---

14 James K.A. Smith, *Desiring the Kingdom* (Grand Rapids, Baker Academic, 2009), 43.

15 LOL, just kidding. I buy all my groceries at Walmart. *Way* better snack selection.

Will that make the book of Numbers your go-to favorite book in the Bible? Probably not. But when you make your way there, you'll see it with fresh eyes.

You'll see how God is teaching his people to love.

And you'll see how Jesus is peeking out from each page, making himself known.

▌▌ A Brief Pause

Digging through dusty rules and regulations sounds about as fun as a root canal, but clearly Jesus considers them to still be important. And what's up with that?

What does Jesus reveal about himself in this section of his sermon?

_____

_____

_____

And what does Jesus reveal about you? What does your response to Jesus' words tell you about yourself?

_____

_____

_____

The notion that God's warnings are a reflection of his mercy—how does that strike you? In what ways does—or doesn't—that sound like the God you know?

_____

_____

_____

_____

Chapter 3

ANGER

You have heard that our ancestors were told, "You must not murder. If you commit murder, you are subject to judgment." But I say, if you are even angry with someone, you are subject to judgment! If you call someone an idiot, you are in danger of being brought before the court. And if you curse someone, you are in danger of the fires of hell.

So if you are presenting a sacrifice at the altar in the Temple and you suddenly remember that someone has something against you, leave your sacrifice there at the altar. Go and be reconciled to that person. Then come and offer your sacrifice to God.

When you are on the way to court with your adversary, settle your differences quickly. Otherwise, your accuser may hand you over to the judge, who will hand you over to an officer, and you will be thrown into prison. And if that happens, you surely won't be free again until you have paid the last penny.

—Matthew 5:21-26

And here I thought this book was going so well.

Being a light to the world and appreciating the First Testament are noble endeavors and, with a little dedication, feel realistically possible.

But then Jesus says if you're angry with someone you're just as bad as a murderer. If that's the case, I don't want to even *consider* how many murders I've committed on my local highways. When I only call other drivers "idiots," I expect a medal for heroism and self-restraint.

Yet Jesus says that puts me in danger of severe judgment.

Here's where the Sermon on the Mount skips straight from "challenging but doable" to "are-you-*kidding*-me impossible" with no stopover at "I'm not so sure about this..."

Which makes this a good time for me to propose the following: I suspect Jesus intends for it to be impossible for his audience to actually live up to these unreasonable standards.

You see, for the previous thousand-plus years, the Jewish people had lived according to the law. And I'm not talking just about the Ten Commandments.

Tradition says Jews in Israel at the time of Jesus had 613 laws to obey.[1] Nobody was able to keep all 613 laws at all times.[2] Yet it wasn't *technically* impossible to do so. That meant people could realistically believe that if they tried really, really hard, they could go for long stretches without violating any law. And even if they couldn't pull off perfection, they'd end up more righteous than they'd started. At least, that was the prevailing thought.

Jesus ends that game.

Think that because you haven't murdered anybody, you've gained a measure of righteousness? You should know that not killing someone isn't the real standard; experiencing unrighteous anger is the standard.

In just a few lines of this sermon, Jesus raises the bar from "don't commit adultery" to "don't lust." And "love your friends and family" is raised to "love everyone, including your enemies."

This, as you may imagine, is terrible, terrible news for any religious person who wants to earn God's favor. It's like they've been playing a pinball tournament for the past thousand years, seeing who can keep the "obeying the law" ball in play the longest. And then Jesus comes along to reset all the records and, while he's at it, removes the flippers.

So why does Jesus do this? Why does Jesus lift the bar from "exceedingly difficult" to "impossible"?

It's because the law, which had been turned into a scoreboard, was never intended to be a pathway to salvation. It was always intended to show us our need for a salvation we can't attain on our own. It was supposed to point toward our need for a Messiah.

---

1   https://en.wikipedia.org/wiki/613_commandments (I know, I know, citing Wikipedia is usually a no-no. Well, this isn't an academic paper, and I felt this article was well sourced and substantiated, so I'm letting it ride.)

2   Romans 3:10; Ecclesiastes 7:20

"Wait," you might say, "then it worked. The Jews were totally looking for a Messiah when Jesus showed up."

Yes, but the Messiah they were looking for was a conqueror who'd throw out the Romans and make Israel powerful and rich again. Religious leaders expected to become even more powerful because of the Messiah. Instead, the Messiah dismantled their system and left them with little political power.

Jesus is drilling beneath the surface of actions to heart. He's making it clear to anyone who listens that the Kingdom of God doesn't operate on the established political power structures or on having the willpower to keep the rules.

The Kingdom requires just one thing: supernatural, Holy Spirit–fueled dependence on God through Jesus.

Because without the Holy Spirit, what Jesus asks of us simply cannot happen.

Imagine you're watching athletes compete at a track and field championship. The world record for the high jump is just over 8 feet, and the competitors regularly clear heights over 7 feet as the crossbar creeps higher with every round.

Then one of the judges comes over and moves the bar up to 20 feet.

No jumper can possibly clear this height. They realize they need something more than what they can do on their own, so poles are brought out so they can vault up and over this terrific height.

This is what Jesus wants to accomplish in his sermon. He wants to prompt that moment when we all realize, "This is completely impossible on my own. I need help getting over that bar."

That help, of course, was the life, death, and resurrection of the very man who's speaking to us on the mountainside. He's the only one who can help us clear the height of his expectations, and God's gracious gift of salvation is the pole that lifts us far higher than we can soar on our own.

Jesus' impossible-to-do expectations force us into relationship with him.

When Jesus declares that we can no longer simply get angry at others but, instead, must care about them and seek to resolve our differences, warning sounds and flashing lights go off in my head.[3]

Those sounds and lights tell me I need the power of the Holy Spirit to make this work.

And, again, I suppose that's exactly Jesus' point.

Before we take a closer look at Jesus' unreasonable expectations—to care, seek forgiveness, and resolve differences—let me briefly point out that all three have to do with creating community.

God's purpose in creating humanity was so we could be in community with God. And God's motivation wasn't that he needed friends; God already exists in community.

---

3   DANGER, WILL ROBINSON! (I told you I was a sci-fi lover.)

You know the whole "One God in Three Persons" idea that's usually called "The Trinity"? That's the God-community, and as God's creations, we've been invited—by God—to enter into our place in that community.

Our sin shuts us out, but through Jesus we're invited in. And that's not the end of it.

We get the opportunity to invite others into the community as well, and the book of Romans tells us that, in his time, God will bring all of creation back into this community.[4]

Our growing community is part of the "Kingdom of God" Jesus talked so much about. It's something we call the "body of Christ."

You and I both know being in community can be challenging. Perhaps that's why Jesus helps us replace the anger in our hearts with what it takes to build healthy relationships and Kingdom community.

I just know this: If you're going to be in community with *me*, it's going to be helpful if you've learned how to forgive. Just saying.

Care about others.

When Jesus tells us to not get angry with or insult others, he's telling us to value people—to see them as more than simply players in our own lives.

When other drivers cut me off in traffic, it's easy to get angry with them. To see them as nothing more than frustrations in my life. But they have value in and of themselves. God put it there.

Scripture's very clear that every human being is made in the image of God.[5] So my caring about others begins by recognizing that God created them, just like he created me.

It's hard to care about people even as they frustrate me. But it's less of a challenge since I began doing something I suggest you try if God's still working on your anger, too.

The next time you're angry with someone, replace "idiot," "jerk," or whatever other insult comes to mind with the phrase "God's image."

When you're driving and have to slam on the brakes because of another driver, shout out, "What is that God's image *doing*?" I find it's harder to be angry when I'm not personifying my anger. When, instead, I put my anger in its proper place.

Yeah, I see that eye roll. I know this seems cheesy, but trust me, it works. You're agreeing with God's truth, and he honors it.

When you talk about people as if they have value, your heart begins falling in line with your actions.

Nazis called Jewish people "rats" during the Holocaust. Hutus called Tutsis "cockroaches" in the Rwandan genocide. You know why? Because it's okay to kill rats. Nobody complains if you step on a cockroach. When we belittle people with our words, it leads to belittling them in our hearts.

---

4   Romans 8:20-21
5   Genesis 1:26

But when you train your heart to respect others, you're able to truly care about them even when they're being inconsiderate.

Seek forgiveness.

God loves giving us regular opportunities to correct unhealthy patterns. For instance, the Apostle Paul suggested never letting a full day go by without resolving feelings of anger.[6]

In this portion of the Sermon on the Mount, Jesus sets the unreasonable expectation that we shouldn't let an occasion to worship go by without resolving any ongoing conflicts of which we're a part—and for which we need forgiveness.

Jesus sees keeping our relationships healthy as a prerequisite to worship, which, at first glance, seems a little crazy to me. What does my relationship with other people have to do with how I worship God?

Apparently, quite a bit.

Jesus wasn't tossing out this concept casually. Consider these Scripture passages:

"In the same way, you husbands must give honor to your wives…Treat her as you should *so your prayers will not be hindered*" (1 Peter 3:7, emphasis added).

"*If someone says, 'I love God,' but hates a fellow believer, that person is a liar*; for if we don't love people we can see, how can we love God, whom we cannot see?" (1 John 4:20, emphasis added).

While I may see my relationship with God as distinct from my relationships with others, Jesus sees them as inextricably linked. Allowing dysfunction to exist between myself and others affects my ability to connect with God.

And the same is true for you.

Healthy engagement with others helps us have a healthy engagement with God.

If there's unresolved conflict in your life, Jesus says you can't ignore it.

When I was still a fairly new believer in Jesus, I was lying on a hotel bed, praying.

I suddenly realized that I held hatred in my heart toward my father.[7] And just as suddenly, I knew God brought this to my attention because he wanted me to deal with it. I immediately called my dad and, for the first time in years, told him I loved him.

It was awkward and difficult at the time, but I'm grateful I made the call and moved the relationship toward restoration. I'd hate to spend the rest of my life letting such an important relationship be continually dysfunctional.

---

6   Ephesians 4:26

7   One way God speaks to me is by guiding my thoughts or bringing a realization to the forefront of my understanding. I learned long ago that God made each of us individually, so God may speak to you in other ways.

Relational healing as described by Jesus in this sermon is at the heart of maintaining community. It's how we reset, how we restore what's bent or broken.

There may be relationships too shattered to ever be restored (abuse comes to mind), but generally speaking, if we're actively seeking to resolve differences rather than throwing away relationships, we're on the right track.[8]

Resolve differences and live graciously.

Another unreasonable expectation of Jesus is that his followers resolve issues before they become legal problems. Which doesn't seem unreasonable at all, frankly. It seems like solid, practical advice.

But there's a principle here that applies beyond the specific situation of legal disputes, and it's this: Jesus is looking for us to function out of graciousness rather than demanding our rights in every situation.

Which I sometimes find very, very difficult.

I'm growing in my ability to say "yes" to Jesus when it comes to his expectation that I not view myself as the center of the universe. Here's an example of how that growth is playing out: When I'm in the express checkout line, I no longer count the items in the cart in front of me.

There was a time I kept track, and if a shopper placed on the conveyer belt even one box of mac 'n' cheese beyond the stated limit of 10 or 20 items, I'd silently seethe with anger at the injustice I was suffering.[9]

Somebody needed to tell that person to *get out of this line*. His actions were an insult to rule-abiding citizens like myself!

Same thing when merging onto a traffic-filled road. I used to feel that anyone zooming up to an obstruction and then trying to merge into my lane at the last moment should be blocked for such rude and inconsiderate behavior.

My point isn't that it's okay for other people to be inconsiderate. My point is that *I'm* learning to be more gracious, to no longer wish justice could be meted out according to my standards.

If somebody in line has a few extra items, it's not the end of the world. A person who merges late on the traffic-congested highway isn't causing me any real inconvenience.

Those occasions now serve as reminders of what Paul wrote in Galatians 6:7: "You will always harvest what you plant."

The seeds I plant today determine what's on my plate tomorrow. Graciousness leads to peace and contentment. Impatience and inconsiderate behavior lead to stress and frustration.

---

8   If you want to look at this topic in some additional depth, Matthew 18:15-20 is a great resource for when you have been offended. *Enemies of the Heart* by Andy Stanley also covers the topic very well.

9   On my worst days, I'd decide that three apples in a bag should count as three items.

Eventually, inconsiderate people have to deal with the results of their actions. So rather than trying to control those people, I focus on the person I might actually be able to control: myself.

I can't decide how others will act, but I can certainly decide how I'll respond to them, and my responses determine what I'm planting and what, eventually, I'll harvest.

To be sure, there are situations in which we *need* to confront others. Forgiving someone who cut me off in traffic is one thing, but what if I see someone mugging a guy on the subway? Should I just shout "I forgive you!" as I keep walking?

How would Jesus have me respond to legitimate concerns about injustice in our society?

Surely Jesus doesn't expect his followers to be silent or ignore the needs of others—someone being mugged, for instance. But Jesus' unreasonable demand about anger colors even how we respond in those situations.

If we allow our anger to drive our engagement, we won't point those situations and conversations toward redemption.

As Martin Luther King Jr. said, "We never get rid of an enemy by meeting hate with hate; we get rid of an enemy by getting rid of enmity."[10]

It was precisely because King sought to confront evil without resorting to anger that he was able to bring a measure of renewal and redemption into a deeply flawed and broken situation.

Whatever our actions, Jesus insists we not be motivated by hate for others. We're to reflect his heart, acting out of love.[11]

Here—like anywhere else we take a close look at what Jesus says— we discover that what might initially strike us as unreasonable is actually anything *but* unreasonable. Resolving differences doesn't weaken us; it places us on a path to a healthier, fuller life.

The life Jesus invites us to live in him.

---

10   Martin Luther King Jr., *Strength to Love* (Minneapolis, Fortress Press, 2010), 48.
11   1 Corinthians 13:1-3

 A Brief Pause

Jesus may be unreasonable, but he certainly understands us. He knows how our blood can boil just beneath the surface, how our smiles can mask what's really going on in our hearts. He knows the power of anger.

When you consider this portion of Jesus' sermon, how do you feel about Jesus? Why?

_____

_____

_____

When you consider this portion of Jesus' sermon, how do you think Jesus feels about you? Why?

_____

_____

_____

Jesus doesn't seem okay with us just burying issues in the backyard and walking away. What conflicts in your life do you need to stop ignoring and work to resolve?

_____

_____

_____

Chapter 4

ADULTERY

*You have heard the commandment that says,
"You must not commit adultery." But I say, anyone
who even looks at a woman with lust has already
committed adultery with her in his heart. So if
your eye—even your good eye—causes you to
lust, gouge it out and throw it away. It is better
for you to lose one part of your body than for
your whole body to be thrown into hell. And if
your hand—even your stronger hand—causes
you to sin, cut it off and throw it away. It is
better for you to lose one part of your body than
for your whole body to be thrown into hell.*

—Matthew 5:27-30

If you thought Jesus was unreasonable when it came to not hating people, get ready—he's pushing the unreasonable pedal straight down to the floorboard.

When it comes to lust, am I *really* supposed to cut out my eye? Do I *really* need to chop off my hand?

In this portion of his sermon, Jesus doesn't just sound unreasonable—he sounds harsh. As in bushy-eyebrowed-lunatic-prophet-screaming-at-the-top-of-his-lungs harsh.

Relax. Jesus isn't expecting anyone listening to actually gouge out an eye or cut off a hand. Rather, he's making a point as forcefully as he can: that sin is more destructive than we can possibly realize. It's worth taking any measure—however unreasonable—to get it out of our lives.

Shane Claiborne and Tony Campolo wrote something I think gets at the heart of what Jesus is saying: "God hates sin because God loves people. And sin hurts people."[1]

Seated on that hillside, looking into the increasingly uncomfortable faces of his audience, Jesus isn't shaming them. Yes, he's talking about sin. But, no, he's not condemning those who hear his words; he's telling them that they have a problem and don't know just how serious it is. He's getting their attention in a big way.

Jesus wants us to have a fulfilling life, one overflowing with joy, peace, and hope. Sin undermines all of that. And if we're unwilling to address the sin in our lives, we won't have the life Jesus wants us to have.

We have skin in the game too. What we do or don't do will have consequences.

Which sounds a *lot* like a lesson I've learned elsewhere in my life.

You see, when I was in high school, I was a pretty good athlete. I ran track and was one of the captains of my varsity baseball team. Like many teenagers, I could run all day without batting an eye.

It took time, but eventually my metabolism slowed down and my muscles no longer seemed to spontaneously generate. This new reality hit me when I was 29 years old and some friends invited me to play a game of pickup basketball. Before we were finished warming up, I was toast. My legs felt like they were full of lead, and I could hardly jog more than a few steps.

I didn't like this new reality, so I pledged to get in shape. This led to some modest exercise for a few weeks before I reverted to lazing around. A few months later I again made a vague pledge to get in shape, and for a week or two my motivation carried me.

It was a good six months later when, at the doctor's office, I discovered my weight was at a new all-time high. I realized I had to either get serious about getting healthier or I'd continue to see a downward trend.

I signed up to run an "adventure race" eight months later and invited friends to run it with me. I'm competitive, and the idea of performing terribly in front of people I knew terrified me. I trained so hard over the next six months that I began setting personal records.

On the day of the race, I beat all my friends and then proceeded to run the mile or so back to our car from the finish line.[2]

---

1   Shane Claiborne and Tony Campolo, *Red Letter Revolution* (Nashville, Thomas Nelson, 2012), 134.
2   Adventure races usually involve obstacles like walls, cargo nets, tunnels, and so on. I've also run races that include dashing through fire, receiving electric shocks, getting tear gassed, and jumping into dumpsters filled with ice water...in winter. If you're wondering what's wrong with me, the short answer is that I suffer from a condition called "awesomeness."

My point: Until I was willing to go "all in"—to sacrifice my desire to be comfortable so I could get back in shape—I didn't make any progress getting where I wanted to be.

There's a story in the Gospels about a rich young man who asked Jesus what he had to do to have eternal life.[3] After a brief conversation, Jesus told the man to "sell all your possessions and give the money to the poor." The young man sadly walked away from Jesus because "he had many possessions."

This may seem like a left turn from a conversation about lust and adultery, but stick with me. I believe they're actually closely related.

Jesus never suggests that all his followers should sell all their belongings and give the money to the poor. Rather, Jesus was putting his finger on the key issue preventing this one man from giving God top priority in his life—an area in which this man didn't want God to be in charge because *he* wanted to be in charge.

And that reluctance? That's sin.

This section of Jesus' sermon makes the same point: Don't let anything be more important to you than having a relationship with God. A relationship in which you're willing to let God be in charge.

When we draw boundary lines for God—"God, you can have everything in my life…except *that*"—we don't experience the full life God wants for us. We settle for second best. Or, in the case of sin, we settle for what looks like short-term gain that actually leads to long-term loss.

The challenge Jesus issues in this portion of his sermon is that we be all-in. That we put God first. That we be willing to cooperate with God as he digs sin out by its roots.

Jesus is letting his listeners know he's serious and checking to see if they're serious as well.

As for me, I've made the choice to be serious about this. And here are four practical ways I've found to cooperate with Jesus as he continues to work on me:

Identify the places in life where Jesus isn't in charge.

There's an easy way to determine where in your life you're not letting Jesus run the show.

It's anyplace you find sin.

It's that spot where you're ignoring God, hoping he doesn't notice what's going on. It's that thing you do or grudge you hold that, as you think about it right now, you feel a twinge of Holy Spirit–inspired guilt.

Got something like that?

Then let me suggest you view that sin the same way you view a warning light suddenly flashing away on the dashboard of your car.

---

3   Matthew 19:16-22

When the oil change light pops on, you know it's time to head to the shop. If the check engine light appears, you'll set up an appointment with the mechanic fast—before something expensive happens.

A while back, that dreaded check engine light came on in my car. It was accompanied by my car bucking like a bronco at a rodeo. Having the automotive-repair skills of a newborn baby hippopotamus, I immediately made for my repair shop.

I knew that if I ignored the warning light (and the other obvious signs something was wrong), things weren't going to get better. If I kept driving my car, I'd do irreparable damage to it.

When we see the warning light of sin in our lives and ignore it, there's a good chance we'll make things worse. That light is an opportunity for us to ask an expert for help, to confess we've found an area of our lives not yet fully given over to Jesus.

And while we can't fix what's broken, Jesus can.

I know we all want to be Chuck Norris in our spiritual growth—blowing things up and making stuff happen—but the heart of the Gospel is that we *can't* do this on our own.[4]

When you sin, rather than think, "I have to try harder to be a better person," try thinking this: "Jesus frees me from this. I need to let Jesus be in charge of this part of my life."

The Apostle Paul knew how difficult the whole all-in-for-Jesus thing was to live out, and he wrote this:

"I have discovered this principle of life—that when I want to do what is right, I inevitably do what is wrong. I love God's law with all my heart. But there is another power within me that is at war with my mind. This power makes me a slave to the sin that is still within me. Oh, what a miserable person I am! Who will free me from this life that is dominated by sin and death? Thank God! The answer is in Jesus Christ our Lord" (Romans 7:21-25).

Paul got it. He wanted to live for Jesus like we want to live for Jesus. But sometimes we revert to the bad old ways from the bad old days, and the imaginary indicator lights on our dashboards start twinkling like a Christmas tree.

Elsewhere, Paul writes that when we allow the Holy Spirit to fill our lives, we'll see results: love, joy, peace, patience, kindness, goodness, faithfulness, gentleness, and self-control.[5]

Not that we can crank out those qualities on our own. That's up to the Holy Spirit. We just need to let the Spirit do it.

When I see sin in my life, it's not a sign that all is lost. It's a reminder that I need to let Jesus give me new life in those places where the sin has taken root.

---

4   This statement should IN NO WAY be taken as a slight upon Chuck Norris. Please don't roundhouse kick me, Mr. Norris.

5   Galatians 5:22-23

In that way, it's actually an *encouraging* thing to spot where lust has its hooks in me, or selfishness, or any other sin.

Now I can turn that over to Jesus.

Accept it—you'll never stop needing God's grace.

Too often in the Christian world, our theology has been "We're bad; God's good; try harder."

Good luck finding a theology more out of line with the Christian Scriptures. What's *actually* in the Bible is this: "We're sinners; God loves us; let's let him forgive, redeem, and restore us."

God's grace isn't a set of training wheels that props us up until we learn to do it all by ourselves. None of us will ever be perfect in this life. We'll *always* rely on God's grace.

But there's a difference between using grace and abusing grace.

Using grace is when we ask for God's help, add our earnest effort to what he gives us, and then ask for forgiveness when and where we fall short.

Abusing grace is saying, "Well, because God's going to forgive me anyway, I'll just do whatever I want."

Using grace centers around Jesus. Abusing grace centers around ourselves.

It's normal to see growth in our lives the longer we follow Jesus, but we'll never stop needing Jesus or relying on grace. We'll never graduate from relying on his forgiveness.

Never.

Jesus' warning about the dangers of sin isn't a call for us to buckle down and try harder to be good. Instead it's a clear call to move closer to and rely on him.

Consider fasting.

I know, it's my least favorite spiritual discipline, too. But it's probably the most important for me as well.[6]

Especially when I'm dealing with sin in my life.

Because fasting may be one of the most misunderstood spiritual disciplines, let's chat about it.

Fasting isn't about punishing ourselves. When we give up food, Facebook, or anything else, it's not to whip ourselves over our failures and shortcomings. It's not that we're hoping if we punish ourselves enough, God won't step in to do the job for us.

Rather, we're creating space for introspection and refocusing our faith in a world of distractions and consumer content that mercilessly seek our attention.

Fasting, in other words, isn't about us being "bad." It's about us being broken and needing the healing that God freely offers.

Nor is fasting a way of earning points with God. When we give up something that brings us pleasure, we're simply making a choice.

---

6   I'm guessing there's a correlation in there somewhere—the fact that I don't want to do it and that I really, really need it.

We're saying, "God, you're more important than this other thing in my life." We're not proving anything to God; we're reminding ourselves who we are, who God is, and what we want our relationship with God to be.

The best part of fasting is that it's ultimately not about what we remove from our lives. It's the opportunity to fill that void in our lives with something better, something life-giving.

Starve yourself to have a better, healthier life—now *that's* some high-quality unreasonability. But there's a method to Jesus' "madness."

Jesus tells a story in the Gospel of Matthew that essentially says that when you're getting rid of junk in your life, you can't just leave an empty gap where the junk was.[7] You have to put something in that space; otherwise you won't benefit from the process.

When fasting from food, use mealtimes as opportunities for prayer or quality family interaction.

If you normally spend hours each day binge-watching TV shows, perhaps you could spend some of that time reading instead or volunteering your time to help others.

Giving up something is a chance to do something better, something healthier…something that gets us moving toward that fulfilling life Jesus invites us to live. Where you used to be self-centered, you can be intentionally generous with God and with other people.

Not doing something is an opportunity, not simply an end unto itself.

And look for opportunities to dig in to growing in the very places you're reluctant to grow. A friend of mine once said, "Discipline becomes desire." I totally identify with this.

I mentioned earlier how I discovered I was out of shape and overweight, so I started running. I hated running, but I wanted the results it would give.

I found that, after some time, even though I didn't have fond feelings about running, I wanted to do it. I created a healthy habit that helped me overcome my inherent preference to be lazy.

Recently, I injured my foot and couldn't run for several months.[8] I was miserable because I started to gain weight again and didn't sleep as well. I knew I was missing out on a better quality of life because I couldn't engage in the discipline of running.

When you truly experience the quality of life Jesus offers, not only will you be willing to lay down the things that distract you from experiencing that life but you'll *want* to do it.

Sin loses its appeal. Your hunger to experience Jesus becomes such a desire that you're willing to do whatever it takes to be with him.

Like fasting.

---

7   Matthew 12:43-45

8   When I was younger, I was like Wolverine, healing from anything in about 24 hours. Now I'm old, so "random, minor pain in foot" can turn into "six-month recovery time." Getting old is not fun. I recommend staying young instead.

Like considering an eye or a hand a small sacrifice as opposed to compromising the life of abundance Jesus wants you to have now and forever.

Take action.

There's an enemy of God's Kingdom at work in this world. Satan (a Hebrew word meaning "the accuser") hates our guts,[9] and any time he can keep people from the abundant life Jesus offers, he'll do it.

As Jesus talks about ripping out eyes and lopping off hands, he's saying this: If we're trapped by the enemy, we're better off cutting away whatever holds us in place than remaining ensnared.

The movie *127 Hours* tells the story of a hiker who became trapped by a boulder. After five days, the hiker decided to amputate his own arm so he could escape what would otherwise become the site of his own death.

Jesus paints sin in the same light: Do whatever you need to do to escape from it. Don't let sin prevent you from experiencing the healing and blessings he offers.

Instead of your eyes or hand, you may find other places in your life where you can metaphorically "gouge" or "cut" out of your life behaviors that have trapped you.

Limiting or filtering the internet in your home may be a healthy sacrifice.

Joining an addiction recovery group may help you get past something that's holding you back from experiencing everything God wants for you.

Setting up a meeting with a counselor to work though hate or an inability to forgive may transform your emotional health.

Again, Jesus is *not* actually wanting you to physically gouge out eyes or cut off hands, because, among other reasons, doing so won't ultimately fix sin. Sin is an issue of the heart.

There's an insanely interesting story in John 5 where Jesus heals a man who has been lying paralyzed for 38 years and then says, "Stop sinning, or something even worse may happen to you" (v. 14).

Call me shallow, but 38 years paralyzed? I think that's about as bad as it gets. And given that he was paralyzed, what sort of sinning had he been doing? Seems to me his options were limited.

But though his eyes and hands weren't sinning, his heart certainly could have been—and apparently was.

Jesus says to that man what he says to us: Take sin seriously. And put nothing off limits in your quest to live in relationship with your Father in heaven.

---

9   Many insights from the scriptural narrative point to this statement being accurate. See Ephesians 6:12 and 1 Peter 5:8 for a couple of brief signposts to this effect.

▌▌ A Brief Pause

Deadly—that's how Jesus views sin. It's worth any price to remove it from your life, to blast away that barrier between you and God.

In this section of Jesus' sermon, what does he reveal about himself? How do you feel about what he reveals?

_____

_____

_____

Jesus is saying something about you, too. What is it? How do you feel about it?

_____

_____

_____

Jesus' story of the rich young man sends a message: Jesus is very willing to put his finger on whatever issue is hurting our friendship with God. Where might Jesus be challenging you to make a change, perhaps even a radical change?

_____

_____

_____

Chapter 5

DIVORCE

You have heard the law that says, "A man can divorce his wife by merely giving her a written notice of divorce." But I say that a man who divorces his wife, unless she has been unfaithful, causes her to commit adultery. And anyone who marries a divorced woman also commits adultery.

—*Matthew 5:31-32*

During the past 2,000 years, Scripture has been used to justify some reprehensible behaviors.

Crusaders in the 11th through 15th centuries found verses in the Bible that encouraged them as they repeatedly attacked Muslims, Jews, and other Christians.

American slave owners in the 18th and 19th centuries used Scripture to justify slave ownership. Even some Christian ministers "owned" slaves, comfortable that Scripture offered them moral grounds to do so.[1]

Men have long used isolated Scripture verses to insist that women should be submissive and subservient to husbands, with less attention paid to how men are to treat their wives.

And this tendency to pull passages out of context or to interpret them in ways that make what we want to do okay isn't a recent invention. Religious people in Jesus' day were just as adept at the sport as we are. In this passage from Jesus' sermon, he's referring to one such effort.

In Jesus' day, like today, there was a range of opinions about what Scripture says about divorce.

---

1   Curtiss Paul DeYoung, Michael O. Emerson, George Yancey, and Karen Chai Kim, *United by Faith* (New York, Oxford University Press, 2003), 107.

Deuteronomy 24:1 says, "Suppose a man marries a woman but she does not please him. Having discovered something wrong with her, he writes a document of divorce, hands it to her, and sends her away from his house." Some rabbis looked at that verse and interpreted it as saying that if a wife committed adultery, a divorce initiated by her husband was acceptable.

But other rabbis saw something different in the passage. They saw an agreement that a man could divorce his wife for *any* reason. Sexual immorality, nagging, poor housekeeping—any and all reasons were sufficient for a husband to hand his wife a divorce decree, pay her a sum of money, and send her on her way.

Jesus' audience knew about the debate. So as Jesus spoke, they understood he was landing firmly on the side of those rabbis who held marriage in high esteem. While regrettable, divorce was permitted in the case of sexual immorality. But divorce because of an overcooked sheep flank? Nope.

Jesus draws a sharp line. Women aren't commodities, meant to be used and then discarded.

We all tend to accept the interpretations of Scripture that line up with how we see the world, and men in Jesus' day were no different. Jesus' insistence that marriage be held in high esteem is sufficiently distressing to the men he's talking to that when he later reaffirms his position, his disciples say, "If this is the case, it is better not to marry!"[2]

In taking this stance, Jesus gives women far more value than their society generally offered in that time and place. By calling men to task for their casual dismissal of wives, he's elevating the role of women.

But perhaps I'm reading too much into this. Maybe Jesus *isn't* addressing the wider issue of gender inequality here. Perhaps he's only addressing one specific social issue—the issue of divorce.

Here's the problem with that position: This isn't an isolated event, and the politics around divorce are linked to Jesus' view of people—women in particular.

Jesus often gives women far more value than society granted them.

In the book of John, chapter 4, Jesus talks with a Samaritan woman at a well. His disciples are stunned into silence when they see him do it[3] because he's crossing both gender and ethnicity lines to have a conversation with her.

As a result of Jesus' interaction with the woman, her entire town is forever changed, with many people coming to believe in Jesus as Messiah.

In the book of Luke, chapter 10, Jesus visits the home of Mary and Martha. Martha grows frustrated as she makes meal preparations because Mary, her sister, sits at Jesus' feet listening to him instead of helping.

Martha asks Jesus to shoo Mary away and into the kitchen, so to speak. But Jesus refuses and not only allows Mary to stay but also *commends* her.

---

2   Matthew 19:10
3   John 4:27

Here's the big deal in all this: At the time, sitting at the feet of a rabbi indicated you were a student of that rabbi. Women weren't allowed to study with rabbis, and yet when Mary presumed to assume that position, Jesus protected her right to do so.

Mary was allowed to be a disciple of Jesus. This is radical, socially offensive progressiveness—acceptance of a woman disciple by Jesus. Even if we say women have different roles from men, women were *not* created as inferior to men.[4]

In the book of John, chapter 8, a woman caught in the act of adultery is brought before Jesus. The crowd that drags her to Jesus insists that according to the law of Moses, she must be stoned.

The crowd is mostly correct. Leviticus 20:10 and Deuteronomy 22:22 both indicate that adultery should be punished by death. But what the crowd seems to have conveniently forgotten is that both Scriptures indicate that the woman *and* the man were to receive this punishment.

A double standard is being held up before Jesus. A couple was caught in the midst of adultery, and the woman alone is to be punished, whereas the man seems to have been given a complete pass.

Jesus refuses to cooperate with this inequality. Instead, he points out the hypocrisy of the men who stand ready to kill the woman at Jesus' feet: their willingness—perhaps even eagerness—to mete out punishment for sin on others without accepting the same standard for themselves. He's insisting on equal punishment for all, or equal forgiveness for all, regardless of gender.

If these incidents described in the Gospels aren't enough to demonstrate Jesus' commitment to uplifting and honoring women, there's also this: All four Gospels specify that women discovered the resurrection and became the first messengers of that good news.

We view this as the Gospel accounts simply reporting the facts. Women showed up at the tomb, saw what had happened, and were witnesses of the resurrection.

But in that culture, having women as witnesses could have compromised the credibility of the resurrection story. That women would play such an important, central role would widely be seen as an embarrassment.

Yet Jesus trusts his message to the women who came upon him in the garden. He cemented them into his story.

There are other passages in the New Testament that have been used to downplay and sideline women in society. And, to be fair, there are passages from both the First and New Testaments that point to the value of women in the faith community.

My goal here isn't to raise or settle all questions around gender equality in our larger culture. It's an important conversation, and we Christians need

---

4   I'm not here to pick a side in the Complementarianism vs Egalitarianism debate. I'm looking for common ground we can all agree on: that men and women are both made in the image of God.

to engage with it—including how we're addressing gender equality within the Christian community.

I'm simply pointing out that Jesus was far more inclusive than his culture found comfortable when it came to accepting outsiders and those who'd been marginalized, including women. Keeping that in mind as we examine what the Bible says may change how we understand passages that speak to the issue.

We have a Savior who never objectified or subjugated women. Not once.

In this portion of his sermon, Jesus speaks clearly about divorce and how men behave in marriage. But he's reflecting Kingdom values that I believe we can apply not just to marriages but also to *any* relationship where there's an opportunity to value people above and beyond what our culture says is "good enough."

Let me suggest four practical ways to practice that value:

Refuse to objectify people.

The philosopher Immanuel Kant argued that people should never be treated as a means to an end but only as an end in and of themselves.[5] That's a succinct way to summarize the truth Jesus presents in his sermon.

To many men living in Jesus' day, women had become a commodity. But in God's Kingdom, *no* person is a commodity. No person's value stops at what he or she can do for you.

While this is true in marriage, it's also true elsewhere in my life. When I'm checking out at the grocery store, it can be easy to forget that the cashier deserves my attention. That the cashier is a person, not just a way to get groceries into bags and a credit card charged for my purchases.

And if I'm nice only to women (or men, in the case of female readers) I consider attractive, I'm turning them into a commodity.

If I treat people with respect only if they can make my life better—a boss, police officer, dentist, or ticket agent, for instance—I'm treating them as the means to an end. A commodity.

Every person, man and woman, is made in the image of God.[6] There are no insignificant people. There are no people unworthy of your respect.

Use your power and privilege to benefit others.

There's a quote that I'll paraphrase that says nearly all people can stand adversity, but if you want to test a person's character, give the person power.[7]

Jesus says that when you have privilege and power, others should be better off because of it.

In the case of divorce, men had been given the right to end a marriage, and many were using it to serve their own selfish desires. Yet Jesus teaches that

---

5   Immanuel Kant, *Groundwork of the Metaphysics of Morals*
6   Genesis 5:2
7   The quote appeared in the Williamsburg Journal-Tribune on March 26, 1931, and is apparently mistakenly attributed to Abraham Lincoln.

power and privilege are best used *not* to please oneself but rather to benefit others: "You know that the rulers in this world lord it over their people, and officials flaunt their authority over those under them. But among you it will be different. Whoever wants to be a leader among you must be your servant, and whoever wants to be first among you must become your slave. For even the Son of Man came not to be served but to serve others and to give his life as a ransom for many" (Matthew 20:25-28).

You have power to affect the lives of everyone you come into contact with—especially those you see frequently, like co-workers and family members.

So we can't let ourselves off the hook. Jesus is talking to us, too.

Be about engagement, not avoidance.

Instead of investing in their marriages, some men listening to Jesus' sermon were happy to cast those relationships aside to pursue something "better." This still happens today, except in our society both men *and* women can hit the eject button.

Jesus doesn't let us run away from broken areas of our lives. Instead, he seeks to redeem and restore those areas. So Jesus helps us face what we'd rather ignore…or escape altogether.

Engagement…not avoidance. That's the Jesus way.

Jesus never promises to make the circumstances around us perfect. Rather, he's committed to healing us so we can influence our circumstances, so we can make things better.

If there's something in your life   perhaps your marriage, your parenting, or where you work—that you're trying desperately to avoid, ask God how he wants to bring redemption and healing in the midst of that situation.[8]

I've found that the situations I hate the most are often the ones in which I end up growing closer to Jesus.

I was once talking with a young man prior to baptizing him during a church service. He told me how he'd had cancer but had just been cleared by his doctors. He was getting baptized to rededicate himself to Jesus out of a deep gratitude.

He told me that while he experienced some dark and difficult days, he wouldn't go back and change them even if he could—because he'd become a completely different man through the situation.

So stop running away. Turn around and face the brokenness. Lean into it. I did this, quite literally, a few years ago.

For some reason during that stretch of time, when I remembered something selfish or stupid I'd done when I was younger, the memory would

---

8   An important note: If you are in a situation that involves abuse or poses any type of imminent danger to you or your family, *please* get out immediately. Get help. Go to a minister, police station, or counselor and keep repeating what's happened until you get help. You can work through redemption and forgiveness and other important spiritual and emotional matters once you are physically safe.

hurt. Literally hurt. I don't know if it was actual physical pain or just pain in my mind, but it *hurt*.

I'd be eating dinner or taking a shower and feel the memory approaching like a tidal wave. There was no way I could stop it. All I could do was clench my teeth and fists, shut my eyes, and wait until the memory faded away.

I couldn't handle thinking about the pain I'd caused or the wrong I'd done to others. It took an agonizingly long time to realize this wasn't part of the healthy life Jesus called me toward.

I decided there had to be something better than letting the past disaster zones of my life derail me whenever they wanted to.

So I resolved to handle the next incoming tidal wave of memory differently. That next time turned out to be a cold winter morning as I hiked across the parking lot from the subway station to my workplace.

I could feel regret, shame, blame, and self-loathing start crashing down on me. But this time, I didn't clench my fists. I didn't steel myself to take the blows until the wave crashed over me and slowly receded away.

Instead, I stopped walking, closed my eyes, and opened my arms as if I were about to give someone a hug. I welcomed the memory of a time I'd acted stupidly and selfishly and had hurt other people.

I remembered all the details, and then I accepted what I had done. My screw-up, my failure, pointed to the fact that I'm not perfect. That I'm in need of a Savior.

My failure pointed to how great the God who loves me is and how deep his love must be to offer me forgiveness and salvation.

Instead of resisting the memory, instead of scrambling to stay safe from feeling bad, I quit letting the memory own me. It became part of my story rather than the secret of "who I really am."

My story is of a flawed, broken human and the God who loves me. Your worst, most painful story isn't who you are. It's a *part* of who you are, yes, but it isn't the last word unless you let it be.

Engage…don't avoid. Engage the situations and people who seem more powerful than you. Less powerful than you. Engage the part of yourself you'd rather not face.

Restore what's broken in your relationships.

Maybe for you it's being generally dismissive of women. Or Muslims. Or rich white guys. Whoever you've written off because of their color, accent, religion, or bank account, rethink your position.

Jesus sacrifices a great deal to create a renewed world. Are you willing to join him, to cooperate with his intent?

Don't answer too quickly, because there's a cost. It may mean giving up your prejudice. Letting him heal your shame. Surrendering a controlling or superior attitude.

I can't answer the question for you, but it's a question worth answering because the ultimate purpose of this life isn't to make ourselves comfortable. It's to be part of the "making all things new again" mission God's launched in this world.

There's no call to love this world as it is, to stand by and accept intolerance, racism, sexism, or pretty much any other ism you care to name. We follow in the footsteps of a crucified and resurrected Messiah—one who isn't done redeeming and reshaping this world. [9]

And—good news here—he's willing to let you help do some of the lifting.

---

9   Notice how I didn't have any funny/snarky footnotes in this chapter? That's because I want to stay married to my wife, thank you very much. I also have two daughters. We'll get back to our regularly scheduled comments after this chapter in which I talk about how awesome women are.

■■ A Brief Pause

Jesus valued women more than his immediate culture seemed to value them. He also valued children highly. Ditto for tax collectors, fishermen, demon-possessed cave-dwellers, and other assorted sinners like…us.

When you consider how Jesus treated women, what does that tell you about him?

_____

_____

_____

Your actions reflect how you do or don't value women (or cashiers or people who can't do anything for you or anyone you come across). What would someone looking at your life conclude about your values, and why? What might Jesus' words be saying to you?

_____

_____

_____

_____

In what ways do you use whatever power or influence you have in life to uplift others?

_____

_____

_____

_____

Chapter 6
VOWS

You have also heard that our ancestors were told,
"You must not break your vows; you must carry
out the vows you make to the Lord." But I say,
do not make any vows! Do not say, "By heaven!"
because heaven is God's throne. And do not say,
"By the earth!" because the earth is his footstool.
And do not say, "By Jerusalem!" for Jerusalem is
the city of the great King. Do not even say, "By
my head!" for you can't turn one hair white or
black. Just say a simple, "Yes, I will," or "No, I
won't." Anything beyond this is from the evil one.

—Matthew 5:33-37

Are you a habitual snooze-button abuser? I certainly am.[1]

Here's what happens: If I have to be up every day at 7:00 a.m., I'll set my alarm for 6:50 so I can hit snooze once. But after a few days or weeks, I get into the habit of snoozing twice. So in order to wake up on time, I change my alarm to start going off at 6:40. After a bit, I decide I like snoozing more than twice, so I need to adjust the starting time of my alarm accordingly.

In my worst cycles, I've gotten to the point where my alarm goes off two or more hours before I actually have to get up. Needless to say, my wife does not generally appreciate this.

At several points in the past, realizing I was trapped in a cycle of almost endless snoozing, I declared snooze-button bankruptcy. I changed my alarm

---

1   You can keep your six-minute abs. I'll take my nine-minute snooze, thank you very much.

to 7:00 a.m. on the dot and vowed to wake up on the first notification…until I decided I deserved one more snooze.

You can imagine the rest.

If you're not a snooze-button abuser, I can picture you shaking your head at how ridiculous this is. I'm costing myself sleep because I keep hitting a button over and over. I'm certainly not helping myself feel more rested or getting any additional sleep.

You're right, but sometimes the cycle just gets the better of me.

I believe the core issue Jesus is pointing at in this section of his sermon is very similar to my snooze-button problem. The people in Jesus' day were in a cycle that had escalated to an extreme and unhealthy place.

But instead of an issue with getting out of bed, the issue was with being transparent and honest.

Instead of making promises that could be counted on to be kept, some people in Jesus' audience had to invoke holy vows to be taken seriously.

"Yesterday I said I'd pay $10 for that tunic you gave me. Today, to get you to believe me, I'll swear by the king and his palace that I'll pay you the 10 bucks. Tomorrow I'll have to double swear by all of heaven and earth that I'll do what I promised, though I clearly haven't followed through already."

The cycle continued until nobody listened unless you were triple swearing on every fiber of your being. Talk was cheap. Vows had become bankrupt, meaningless.

Fast forward to today.

Has talk ever been cheaper than in this age of social media and 24-hour cable "news" networks?

We can all participate on platforms that let us share opinions and experiences, tell jokes, post stories, put up pictures and video, and on and on. My social network feed currently includes discussions about politics, movies, faith, music, births, deaths, news stories, food, and pretty much every other topic under the sun.

We can also tune in to a television channel at any hour of the day or night to watch others share opinions about…anything.

And in the midst of this constant barrage of broadcasting we seem, as a society, to have lost our ability to hold respectful conversations. Disagree with my viewpoint and you're not only wrong but also stupid and evil.[2] We live in a climate where we're almost obliged to attack and destroy any opinions that aren't in line with our own.

This is clearly *not* in alignment with how Jesus approaches even his staunchest adversaries.

---

2   I'm not calling you stupid and evil. I'm saying that's how we're being trained by segments of our society to view people who disagree with us. You, dear reader, are smart and wholesome. Also, quite good-looking. In fact, have you lost weight recently? I noticed it earlier but didn't want to say anything until it made sense in the conversation. Beyond that…your breath? Minty fresh.

This section of Jesus' sermon doesn't actually appear to be unreasonable, does it? It's *reasonable* to expect someone who makes a promise to keep it. It's *reasonable* that when we say we'll do something, we'll do it.

Yet we're often taken by surprise when a company makes good on a promise. When a salesperson is completely transparent and honest about a product. When someone in court tells the truth, the whole truth, and nothing but the truth.

Jesus tells his followers to be people who tell the truth, who have no need to artificially inflate their credibility with vows.

To be…well, like Jesus himself.

Consider how Jesus handled telling the truth in some very challenging situations:

Jesus and religious leaders

The vast majority of Jesus' arguments were with religious leaders. On more than one occasion, they demand to know where Jesus gets off telling people something different from what the leaders themselves teach.[3]

So Jesus tells them—and he tells them the truth.

Jesus replies that his authority comes from God and that the proof is found in his message, in the miracles that accompany his message, and in witnesses like John the Baptist.[4]

Jesus doesn't take oaths to validate himself. Instead, he points to what he does and the results of his message and actions. In other words, "the proof is in the pudding."

When we buy a house, before we sign a contract, we hire a home inspector to assess the home for us. The reason is simple: While the house may *appear* to be wonderful, we need to know if there's anything we can't see that we need to be aware of. Do the pipes work? Is the sewer system up to snuff? Do the heating and air conditioning function correctly? Is the foundation solid?

If the homeowners start promising on all their dead relatives—even on the ones who aren't feeling well—that their house is a great deal, I still wouldn't waive the inspection. Truth needs no decoration, but rather the opposite: It's deception that must clothe itself in attractive disguises.

Jesus doesn't want us to take our cues from social norms but rather to be countercultural. To speak simple truth in a world of constructed narratives, clever marketing, and, all too often, deliberate deception.

Consider: We followers of Jesus are called to spread the message of the Gospel. It's the most incredible narrative the world has ever heard, bar none.

I'll recap it briefly so we're on the same page here: The God who created us and who knows everything about us—every action, thought, and word—loves us. He's paid a great personal price so our broken relationships—with God and others—can be restored.

---

3   Luke 20:1-2
4   John 5:31-38

Yet, many times, followers of Jesus have relied on manipulation, condescension, and half-truth marketing tricks to share this narrative.

Jesus himself never resorts to cheap tactics or insincere patronizing to spread his message of truth. Rather, he engages in conversations, and that's when people open up to new perspectives and viewpoints.[5]

Jesus' words are always for the benefit of his hearer, never for his own benefit. How's that for an unreasonable expectation for us to follow?

Even when Jesus is seen arguing, it isn't about stroking his own ego. If anything, Jesus' arguing with the religious leaders of his day is an effort to hold them back so he could minister to the outcasts of society without man-made rules and regulations getting in the way.

To say that even more bluntly: Jesus argues religion only to protect everyone else from the religious leaders of his day.

We as Christians can take a cue from Jesus. As Robert Capon argues, the church should never be in the religion business but rather in the Gospel-proclaiming business.[6]

In the places where we have a problem with our culture, let's have the courage to do what Jesus did: *Have a conversation about it.*

When Christians use impersonal mass communications (social media, television/radio, and billboards come to mind) as a way to offer broad, nonrelational criticism to the general public, I believe we're violating the model Jesus gave us.[7]

It's my belief that in this section of the Sermon on the Mount, where Jesus talks specifically about vows, he's letting us know we can't rely on cheap tricks to gain an audience. Honest, authentic communication allows us to form genuine relationships, and it's through those kinds of relationships that the Gospel can be effectively shared.

What was at the heart of Jesus' problem with people taking vows?

I think it's this: People in his culture were dragging God into their vows, with an eye on increasing their own credibility.

We still do it. When you hear someone "swear on my mother's life" (Never heard that? Watch a few TV movies about life in the mafia. Apparently Mafiosi talk like that all the time.[8]) that they're telling the truth, it's saying, "You have

---

5   Consider, as an example, the conversation Jesus had with Nicodemus. John 3:1-21 outlines the conversation. John 7:50-52 shows that this conversation caused Nicodemus to, at the very least, extend Jesus the opportunity to prove his claims.

6   Robert Farrar Capon, *Kingdom, Grace, Judgment* (Grand Rapids, Wm. B. Eerdmans Publishing Co., 2002), 177.

7   I'm only talking about criticism here. If a church wants to advertise and invite people through social media, billboards, TV, and/or radio, I'm not only okay with that, but I totally support it. I'm thinking of billboards telling people they're going to hell or social media posts blasting the immorality of certain people or groups. That approach, in my viewpoint, is quite contrary to how Jesus interacted with others.

8   Am I right or am I right? Fuhgeddaboudit.

to believe me because I'm appealing to something more valuable than the words I'm saying."

The people listening to Jesus weren't doing that with Mom…but with God, and Jesus is calling it out as a problem.

First, God is never content to be just a rubber stamp on our own decisions.

Second, Jesus values integrity. Saying what you mean and meaning what you say. Being a person of your word. Jesus saw that insincere vows undermined healthy communication and asked us to do something better. Something healthier.

No wonder Jesus gets impatient with hearing God used as a prop to manipulate conversations. It's something Jesus didn't do, and if anyone had the right, it's Jesus.

Making a vow in an effort to increase your credibility isn't the way to prove you're telling the truth. Holier sounding words don't mean you have integrity. Jesus tells the truth—always. He was and *is* the Truth. And his unreasonable expectation is that we'll be like him.

Even when we're in hard situations. Even when others doubt us and our word. Even when adding a vow might somehow get us clear of conflict. For Jesus, the ends don't justify the means. Doing unhealthy things to get healthy results is a shortcut he didn't allow for himself, and neither will he let us pull that stunt.

It's good news that Jesus not only suggests that level of integrity but also demonstrates it. Since Jesus always put his teachings into practice, let's see how his commitment to being truthful played out in some challenging moments in his life on earth.

Jesus and telling the truth to Herod

When hauled before Herod, the ruler of Jerusalem, Jesus remains silent. Luke reports that Herod asks questions—lots of them—and hopes to see Jesus perform a miracle.[9] But Jesus doesn't say a word.

In what way is that telling the truth?

Jesus recognizes that Herod's questions aren't coming from a place of genuine curiosity or respect. Herod isn't interested in learning about God; he simply wants to be entertained.

And Jesus refuses to play along.

In some situations, simply remaining silent is the most truthful response possible. There's a big difference between sharing with someone who's sincerely engaged and dealing with someone who isn't really interested in having a conversation.

I'd go so far as to say it's best to avoid engaging when constructive conversation isn't welcome. There's not much benefit in trying to talk with people who only want to argue for the sake of arguing.

---

9   Luke 23:8-9

The most genuine, truthful interaction Jesus could have with Herod was to refrain from speaking to him. Sincere words to the wrong ears aren't useful.

I've had the pleasure of publishing quite a few articles on various well-read websites. On occasion, I'm shredded by people who read an article (or even just its title) and choose to disagree with me.

Now, don't get me wrong. I have no problem when people disagree with me. In fact, I heartily respect other viewpoints. I'm not so narcissistic as to think I'm *always* right.[10]

One goal of my writing is to provide a distinct perspective and hopefully spark thought and introspection. I'm trying to do that right now. With you.

Any time a person messages me directly to discuss or debate a topic I write about, I happily engage. I have this crazy idea that people, and Christians especially, need to be relational, even through the internet.

Unfortunately, what people usually post online is that I'm incompetent, delusional, or idiotic. Sometimes I let that sort of unhealthy comment go, saddened that it's all another person is willing to offer. Other times, I reply and attempt to start a respectful conversation.

But what I *never* do is fight fire with fire by trying to "win" an argument by tearing down the other person. Attacking someone online isn't truth-telling; it's anger. Or contempt. Or maybe even hate.[11]

Jesus' silence with Herod says volumes.

And his encounter with Herod isn't the only place Jesus makes use of selective silence. He largely remained silent regarding political issues, choosing to remain on message and mission rather than be drawn into partisan debates. When crowds wanted to galvanize behind Jesus and back him in a political power grab, Jesus simply walked away from them.[12]

Which is *not* to imply that Christians can comfortably shirk engagement with their civil governments. The early church's message that "Jesus is Lord" was no small political statement, as it could be (and was) interpreted as treasonous.

"Son of God" was imprinted on Roman coins of the time to remind those living in the Empire that Caesar was the highest authority in their lives.[13]

Roman Christians declared that they wouldn't live under such an expectation. Jesus was Lord, not Caesar. Yet even then Paul wrote that Christians should submit to government authorities and pay taxes to the occupying regime.[14]

---

10 I'm sure I'm wrong at least 0.005 percent of the time.
11 This is why I never click on an internet link that is titled along the lines of "MUST WATCH: Argument of Person A DESTROYING Position of Person B."
12 John 6:15
13 N.T. Wright explores this topic deeply in *Paul and the Faithfulness of God* (p. 279), *Simply Jesus* (p. 60), and *Simply Christian* (pp. 117-118).
14 Romans 13:1-7

Even when our governments disappoint or take stances we can't in good conscience support, we're to treat them as honestly as we treat people. To have the same integrity dealing with our taxes as we do with our neighbors.

And to speak the same genuine, truthful words no matter who's president, king, or prime minister.

Jesus telling the truth to Pilate

When Jesus is brought before Pilate, who's acting as both judge and jury in Jesus' trial, Jesus doesn't remain silent. Perhaps that's because Pilate's questions aren't just surface talk, as was the case with Herod.

Jesus answers Pilate's questions: Are you the King of the Jews? Why have your own people brought you to me?

In fact, the *only* time Jesus remains silent is when given a chance to refute the charges brought against him by religious leaders. And Jesus not responding shocks Pilate.[15]

It's possible Jesus doesn't respond because he doesn't disagree with their charges that he's claimed to be the Son of God. Yes, that happened. It was the truth.

It's also possible that Jesus doesn't feel the need to defend himself, instead trusting that God will make clear who's right in the situation.

Pilate may have had civic and judicial authority over Jesus in the moment, but God is still the ultimate authority. Jesus' silence may simply reflect his understanding, acceptance, and trust in that truth.

So, following Jesus' lead, maybe it's not always our job to defend ourselves when our honesty is questioned or we're falsely accused. Instead we can allow God to defend us.[16]

Remember, while Pilate *appears* to have power over Jesus in the moment, thousands of years later we worship Jesus and view Pilate as having landed on the wrong side of God's plan for this world.

In those pivotal moments in front of Pilate, Jesus doesn't argue. Rather, he states the truth and accepts the decisions of those who've been given authority to make decisions.

Try *that* on for unreasonable.

Hard truth: Often, our best opportunity to demonstrate the transformed life we've been given is to respond calmly and respectfully in the face of injustice and disrespect.

The result of Jesus speaking truth was persecution. That's still a common outcome.

---

15 Mark 15:3-5
16 Bonus unreasonable content: not defending yourself when others make unjustified accusations against you. To those of us who have a strong "justice streak," this may feel like Jesus just turned the "unreasonable" knob up to 11.

Think of American civil rights protesters in the 1960s. Through both word and deed these brave people addressed injustice. The result: insults, beatings, and, too often, death. Persecution.

When we embrace Jesus' unreasonable expectation that we'll speak plain truth, we have to be prepared for the likelihood that not everyone will appreciate what we say.

America today is far from perfect, but it's better because of the actions of civil rights protesters who refused to argue and insult but rather had the courage to bear the impact of hate and injustice. All because they called hate and bigotry for exactly what it was.

They told an unpopular truth and stood by what they'd said.

How do we do the same? How do we gain a reputation as truth-tellers like Jesus was a truth-teller, one who doesn't need a vow to be judged as authentic and having integrity?

Let me suggest three ways:

Be humble.

Jesus challenges the idea that we're ultimately in control.

Whether I say "yes, I can raise the money," or I vow "yes, by the power of Grayskull, I can raise that money," I'm still a human. There are limits to what I can control, vow or not.

We can swear by the heavens and the earth, but we have no control over either. God's ultimately in control, which is a good thing because he promised to make all things new.

Our words need to mean something. When Jesus tells people their sins are forgiven, he doesn't do so through long, flowery speeches. When he tells them to go and sin no more, he doesn't add a long list of consequences. He says what he has to say, simply and compassionately, even when confronting others.

Let's follow his example.

Be trustworthy.

At the core of what Jesus says in this section of the Sermon on the Mount is a caution: If you have to add anything to the simple truth to be believed, there's a problem.

Our reputation as Christ-followers needs to be that we can be trusted. Not that we're perfect but that we don't endorse our society's loose relationship with the truth. Rather, we're following the healthier example of our Messiah.

When we honor Jesus' advice to "say what we mean and mean what we say," we become people who others can trust.

Be a listener.

When people disagree with us, there's seldom a need to escalate by countering their words with even more powerful words of our own. Instead, discover the joy of simply asking for someone's story and seeking to understand.

That's where the good stuff happens because it leaves space for God to work through us. That's when we can both rely on God's grace and share it with others.

Jesus talks about using our worldly resources to gain friends so we can all enjoy God's eternal community.[17] I'd suggest that among those worldly resources are our social interactions. When you listen, when you help someone feel cared about, you're building a relationship that can point toward the hope you have in Jesus.

But this is important: Don't listen just until you get an opening to share your faith in Jesus. Rather, listen because God said to love people and create community wherever possible.

As the authors of *The Art of Neighboring* write, "We don't love our neighbors to convert them; we love our neighbors because we are converted."[18]

When I'd just become a believer in Jesus, I tried to tell everyone in my school about my new faith. After all, I had discovered the Truth and I wanted to share it!

My intentions were good, but I quite possibly did more harm than good because I didn't understand that valuing others was more important than telling them what to think.

In pottery class one day,[19] another student was refuting my claims of faith, and in a moment of complete frustration I said, "Have fun in hell when I'm waving at you from heaven!"

He laughed and we stayed friends, but it was probably the dumbest thing I've ever said. I was an arrogant jerk who didn't yet realize I have no authority to make decisions about who's in heaven and who's in hell. Since then, I've learned to listen more and I've become humbler, turning down the dial a bit on my sarcasm.

But like everyone else I know (I'm thinking of you), I'm still a work in progress.

In listening...in being trustworthy...in humility...in simply sharing the truth.

---

17 Luke 16:9
18 Jay Pathak and David Runyon, *The Art of Neighboring* (Grand Rapids, Baker Books, 2012), 102.
19 Like you've never taken a class because it was going to be an easy A.

 # A Brief Pause

You know, this doesn't *really* have to be a brief pause. You can take whatever time you need to consider these questions. Honest. No hurry.

What does this portion of his sermon tell you about Jesus?

_____

_____

_____

_____

As you read what Jesus said, what do you discover about yourself?

_____

_____

_____

_____

Jesus is encouraging us to be trustworthy—to do what we say we'll do. Would you say your reputation is one of trustworthiness? Why do you answer as you do?

_____

_____

_____

_____

Chapter 7

REVENGE

*You have heard the law that says the punishment
must match the injury: "An eye for an eye,
and a tooth for a tooth." But I say, do not resist
an evil person! If someone slaps you on the
right cheek, offer the other cheek also. If you
are sued in court and your shirt is taken from
you, give your coat, too. If a soldier demands
that you carry his gear for a mile, carry it
two miles. Give to those who ask, and don't
turn away from those who want to borrow.*

—Matthew 5:38-42

Revenge is a concept as old as humanity itself: If you do me wrong, then I deserve to pay you back in kind.

And this isn't just cave man stuff. We may still find ourselves muttering "I owe him one" when we think we've been done wrong.

But here, Jesus says we shouldn't seek revenge, even when someone has clearly done something to us. Instead, Jesus says *not* to seek to balance the ledger sheet.

Why does Jesus ask us to simply accept poor treatment? to turn the other cheek and let it slide?

Simple. Because he wants us to replace revenge with justice.

Justice is a wonderful concept. It means all wrongs have been set right. Everyone is even, and everything is fair.

You'd think reasonable people would welcome a world that's fair for all, that by now we'd have sorted out a way to ensure justice.

But this world is *not* just. In fact, it's painfully obvious that, at least in our time, our world falls far short of that standard.

It's not that we don't try. Most countries, and a handful of multinational or global organizations, have developed judicial systems designed to deliver justice. To make sure—as Jesus mentions—that punishments match the injuries sustained.

Yet every one of those judicial systems often comes up short in delivering justice.

Some people who commit crimes are never caught, and it's unjust that anyone should be able to avoid the consequences of their criminal activity.

It's also unjust that some innocent people suffer for crimes they didn't commit. During the past 20 years or so, in the U.S. alone, new DNA testing has resulted in more than 300 people being freed from prison. [1]

Some of those innocent people were on death row before being completely exonerated.

And the problems don't end there. Beyond unjust verdicts, there's unjust sentencing. If you kill someone and are sent to prison, how long should you be incarcerated?

Depending on the details (Were you defending yourself? Was it an accident? Were you being reckless? Was the victim a police officer or government official?), you may be sentenced to death, you may be released almost immediately, or you may be punished in a way that falls between those extremes.

In 2014, a Texas teenager killed four people in a drunk-driving accident and was sent to a rehab center and then put on probation rather than doing time in jail. That sentence prompted significant public outrage.[2]

On the other hand, in 2012, more than 3,000 people in the American penal system were serving life sentences without the possibility of parole for nonviolent crimes involving drugs or property.[3]

How does *that* add up? Kill four and serve probation while down the road in a state prison, someone who didn't take even one life serves out his or her remaining lifetime behind bars?

I mention this apparent inconsistency to make a simple point: We humans are seldom good at implementing justice—legally or otherwise.

At the time Jesus delivered this sermon, the concept of "an eye for an eye and a tooth for a tooth" was considered the purest form of justice.

And yet Jesus says that equation simply doesn't work.

Jesus isn't dismissing the idea of justice. At the very outset of the Sermon on the Mount, Jesus says, "God blesses those who hunger and thirst for justice, for they will be satisfied" (Matthew 5:6).[4]

---

1   http://www.innocenceproject.org/dna-exonerations-in-the-united-states/
2   Google "Texas teen affluenza"
3   Google "living death LWOP"
4   Some translations say "hunger and thirst for righteousness," but the NLT brings out the idea that this is connected with the concept of justice.

So how can we reconcile Jesus' expectation that we hunger and thirst for justice with his expectation that we make peace with living with injustice? Isn't that what he's saying when he asks us to turn the other cheek? To offer a coat along with a shirt that's taken from us?

Those two challenges—to seek justice and be okay when justice isn't served in our own lives—seem to be contradictory.

It's a contradiction that, when I was a teenager, I resolved by deciding that if I wanted justice to be served, I should sometimes shelve Jesus' expectation that I treat others the way I want to be treated. Instead, I should treat those inconsiderate jerks the way they're treating *me*.

I mean, how else could they learn?

I distinctly remember telling my mother about a kid who was being mean to me, and she suggested I forgive him. I told her that for our world to work, the buck had to stop somewhere—and it was going to stop with me.

The very idea of me, as a teenager, bringing justice to everyday life is laugh-out-loud stupid.[5] But my desire to make the world just—at least according to *my* notion of justice—is something I bet we've all wrestled with.

So how do the unreasonable expectations of Jesus help us resolve our frustrations with how justice does—or doesn't—play out in our world?

Here's the key: Jesus doesn't order us to *create* justice. He tells us to hunger and thirst for it.

He's actually calling us to recognize that only God is able to provide true justice.

Why? Because, simply put, we don't know what's just.

Our efforts at justice nearly always amount to retribution at best, sometimes even revenge, and often lead to more injustice.

Who should be punished, and who should be set free? How harsh or light should a sentence be? Ask 10 people what's just punishment for a particular criminal and you'll likely receive 10 different answers.

Even then, if the people being given consequences feel they're not receiving justice, they may seek to even things out. Think Hatfields and McCoys here. Both sides had legitimate grievances, but each felt the other side *owed* them something. When the Hatfields decided to even up the score, the McCoys viewed that action as widening the deficit.

Their disagreement over what justice looked like launched a cycle of retribution. Of revenge.

Only God is able to see the full picture, to examine the hearts of all involved. Only God can truly render justice.

As Miroslav Volf writes in his book *Exclusion and Embrace*, "God treats different people differently so that all will be treated justly."[6]

---

5   Although, on the upside, weekends would have immediately become six days long.

6   Miroslav Volf, *Exclusion and Embrace* (Nashville, Abingdon Press, 1996), 222.

Remember the parable Jesus told about vineyard workers?[7] The owner of a vineyard goes to the market and hires day laborers to work his land. He agrees to pay them a day's wage for a day's work.

Throughout the day, the owner repeatedly returns to the market, hiring additional help. His final visit is only an hour before the workday is done, and he hires a group of people who've been in the market all day but haven't been hired by anyone else.

When it's time to get paid, the workers line up in order, starting with the ones who worked the least amount of time. When the owner gives a full day's wage to the workers who only put in an hour, those who'd worked all day get excited. If people who'd worked only an hour got a full day's wage, how much more would those who worked a full day get?

As it turns out, they get…wait for it…a full day's wage. Exactly what they'd agreed on from the start. But they are *miffed*, and I can understand why. I worked *way* harder than that guy, so why did he get the same as I did?

The point of the story is that, to us, justice looks like this: A person who works longer than another person should get more money. But to God, justice looks like this: Those who worked less through no fault of their own will receive the same as those who worked all day.

Two very different definitions of what's just and fair.

Given that our attempts to be just are, at best, inadequate, how can we cooperate with God's efforts to move us past retribution and revenge and closer to his heart for justice?

Glad you asked. I suggest this:

Create space for God to give justice.

The Apostle Peter wrote, "Don't repay evil for evil. Don't retaliate with insults when people insult you. Instead, pay them back with a blessing. That is what God has called you to do, and he will grant you his blessing" (1 Peter 3:9).

A man once got in my face, screaming and cursing, outside a grocery store. He didn't like that I'd walked across the same space in which he wanted to reverse his car so he could leave the parking lot. Reverse from where he was illegally parked, by the way.

In that moment, I could have sought justice by evening the score: screaming and cursing back at him. Or, since he started it, maybe justice meant escalating the conflict to the next level?[8]

Instead, I stood my ground, waited for him to finish, and then said "God bless you, friend" as he stormed away.[9]

---

7   Matthew 20:1-16
8   By this, I of course mean turning it into a tickle fight.
9   In the middle of the encounter, when he finally took a breath, I tried to de-escalate the incident by saying, "You know, as a pastor, I don't usually have people talk to me in this manner." He cussed me out even more and threatened to kill me. To be honest, it was kind of funny in the moment because of how ridiculous it was.

I didn't argue with him because it wouldn't have done any good. Any effort on my part to gain justice would have been ineffective because he believed I'd already done him harm by inconveniencing him. In his mind, his tantrum was just—he was making things even.

I blessed rather than cursed him because, as Billy Graham has said, "It's the Holy Spirit's job to convict; it's God's job to judge; and it's our job to love."[10]

I acknowledged God's sole ability to bring justice into that parking lot by not assuming I could take God's place in that situation.

Choose to love instead of enforcing imperfect justice.

I want to be very clear about something: I'm not suggesting people shouldn't suffer consequences for crime. If someone steals your car, there should be a penalty for that.

While our justice system is flawed, I'm not advocating that we abandon it—I'm simply suggesting that we understand our shortcomings and that we recognize that our hope for justice is rooted in our faith in God.

But even in the midst of supporting consequences for crime and sin, shouldn't our reaction be somehow different because we follow Jesus?

The story of Mary Johnson and Oshea Israel is a stunning example of how that can be powerfully true.

When he was a teenager, Oshea murdered Mary's son. Oshea was captured, convicted, and sent to prison—a significant consequence for his actions.

Twelve years into Oshea's sentence, Mary's faith prompted her to visit him in prison.[11] She wanted to know whether he'd changed or was still the angry, defiant kid she'd seen in the courtroom.

What she found was a man who deeply regretted what he'd done.

Mary forgave Oshea.

Forgave him—the person who'd murdered her son.

And when Oshea was released from prison, Mary threw him a welcome home party. They're now literally next-door neighbors, and together they speak about their experience.[12]

Oshea and Mary talk about one another as mother and son.

It's hard to claim that justice has been done in this situation. It wasn't. Forgiveness and grace got in the way.

Mary and Oshea chose love, trusting God to provide the justice.

---

10   www.charismanews.com/us/41684-billy-graham-a-faithful-witness

11   Mary writes about this at http://theforgivenessproject.com/stories/mary-johnson-oshea-israel-usa/. While her faith prompted her to forgive, it was not instantaneous; it took time and courage on her part. All the more reason to be in awe of what she did.

12   Visit https://storycorps.org/listen/mary-johnson-and-oshea-israel/ to hear them share their story.

Remember how Jesus faced great injustice.

When Jesus was illegally and improperly tried, convicted, and sentenced to death, he faced a great injustice with great sacrifice.

Jesus could have stopped the injustice at any moment.[13] He chose to make his sacrifice so God could bring something better into this world.

Not long ago, I took my daughter to the Smithsonian Museum of American History. We were able to see the lunch counter from the Woolworth store in Greensboro, North Carolina, where a student sit-in occurred during the American civil rights movement.

Young students who took part in the movement stood up to violence in the manner of Jesus—with a willingness to sacrifice. Some were beaten, mauled by dogs, or blasted with firehoses. Some were even killed.

It certainly feels unreasonable for Jesus to ask me to suffer physical pain because of the unjust behavior of others, but Jesus isn't asking me to do anything he isn't willing to endure himself.

And let's be honest, Jesus' torture and death is far more unjust than anything I'll ever deal with, no matter how severe.

Decide there is no "us" versus "them."

Maybe you've heard the phrase "hate the sin and love the sinner." It seems like a ridiculous concept until you realize, as C. S. Lewis pointed out, we've been doing it all along for at least one person: ourselves.[14]

It's dangerously easy to fall into the habit of judging others for their actions while judging ourselves based on our intentions, regardless of what we actually do.

If we're readily willing to call down "justice" on others but only "grace" for ourselves, we do well to remember that Jesus promises (warns?) that it's the standard we apply to others, not ourselves, that will be applied to us when our lives are sized up.[15]

There's a well-known story about the Christian author G. K. Chesterton that may or may not be true. If it's not true, it should be.

The story reports that a newspaper editor once wrote to Chesterton asking him to submit an essay on the topic "What is wrong with the world today?"

Chesterton's response was brief:

Dear Sir,

I am.

Sincerely,

G. K. Chesterton[16]

---

13   Matthew 26:53
14   C.S. Lewis, *Mere Christianity* (New York, HarperCollins Publishers), 117.
15   Particularly Matthew 6:12 and 7:2, both of which are part of the Sermon on the Mount and will come up later in this book.
16   While no direct references have been found, chesterton.org confirms it may well be an accurate story.

We are all in need of God's grace.

If those of us who have accepted God's grace behave as if we're superior, we're kidding ourselves. If we believe we have the inside track on deciding what's just for everyone else, we're wrong.

We were rescued, and our lives were interrupted by grace and forgiveness. That's not a license to think we're now qualified to judge everyone else we come into contact with.

When we see someone living without having yet accepted Jesus' forgiveness, let's respond with compassion, not righteous indignation.[17]

It's hard to accept this challenge being tossed our way by Jesus.

We *hate* letting people "get away" with being selfish, sinful, or criminal. And I'm not advocating that we encourage such behavior or turn a blind eye to it. Jesus wasn't soft on holding people accountable for sin in their lives either.

But Jesus still calls us to trust God with justice, which in turn frees us to live with compassion.

When we're wronged, we can choose to take matters in our own hands and get what we're able to extract as repayment, or we can allow God to compensate us for our losses.

But we must choose one. We can't have it both ways.

The next time someone steals your lunch at work, cuts you off on the highway, or does something far worse, before you act, pause. Bring your righteous desire for justice to God rather than making demands of other people. Let your hunger and thirst for justice be fulfilled by the only One who can best provide what you seek.

---

17 Listen, I know some readers will immediately think (or possibly shout out loud), "What about child molesters? terrorists? murderers?" It's a valid question. Let's talk about it more in the next chapter.

▋▋ A Brief Pause

Revenge and justice—what might Jesus be saying to you about how both of these play out in your life? Consider these questions:

In what situations do you find yourself most drawn to wanting to take revenge? Why do you think that's the case?

_____

_____

_____

What do Jesus' words about revenge and justice tell you about him? What does your response to his words tell you about you?

_____

_____

_____

What's a place in our world where you sense in yourself a hunger for justice? What—if anything—are you doing to help bring justice?

_____

_____

_____

_____

Chapter 8
LOVE YOUR ENEMIES

You have heard the law that says, "Love your neighbor" and hate your enemy. But I say, love your enemies! Pray for those who persecute you! In that way, you will be acting as true children of your Father in heaven. For he gives his sunlight to both the evil and the good, and he sends rain on the just and the unjust alike. If you love only those who love you, what reward is there for that? Even corrupt tax collectors do that much. If you are kind only to your friends, how are you different from anyone else? Even pagans do that. But you are to be perfect, even as your Father in heaven is perfect.

—Matthew 5:43-48

How much do you love the members of a terrorist group?

Or the latest person who shot up a school, church, or movie theater?

Looks like *this* will be a fun chapter, doesn't it?

Let me say right up front that "love your enemies" is among the most unreasonable things Jesus ever said—maybe *the* most unreasonable.

And that's saying something because it's coming from a guy who also said stuff like "eat my flesh and drink my blood," "hate your mother and father," and "sell all your possessions and give the money to the poor."[1]

But love your enemies? Come *on*.

A brief reminder: When Jesus gives us an unreasonable standard…

---

1   John 6:56; Luke 14:26; and Matthew 19:21 respectively

1. He's not expecting us to do it on our own. We need the Holy Spirit in our lives to meet his expectation. Earlier I described how a pole vaulter needs help clearing a bar set at 20 feet. This expectation hovers more at the 200-foot mark, so we definitely need help. We can't clear it on our own.

2. Jesus loves us and wants us to have a fuller, healthier, better life. So if he tells us to do something difficult, it's in our own best interest to listen to him.

Okay, that's it for the review. Now let's dive in and consider how we can do what Jesus tells us to do: Love our enemies.

My first question is whether the people listening to Jesus when he delivered his sermon could possibly relate to the kind of enemies that exist in our world today: terrorists, mass murderers, and the like.

The answer to that question is an unequivocal "yes."

Jesus and his audience lived under an oppressive occupying Roman government that gleefully employed torture and murder to keep people in line. Everyone within earshot of Jesus had plenty of "I hate you with every ounce of my guts" enemies in the persons of soldiers and prefects carrying out this daily social domination.

So when we talk about applying Jesus' words to more than just the occasional arrogant idiot who pops up in our lives, Jesus' audience could identify.

We're not just talking about the lady who pulls up at 6:00 a.m. in front of the house two doors down and honks the horn[2] or the guy who leaves his dog barking outside until midnight every night.

We're talking about the "I hate you with every fiber of my being, and if I could kill you and get away with it, I'd do it" enemies. Those are the enemies Jesus is telling us to love.

And it seems that Jesus doesn't leave us any wiggle room on this one. He truly wants us to love people who do horrible things. But that doesn't mean we won't try to get out of it.

Because it just doesn't feel right. It's not reasonable. And, inspirational sermon illustrations aside, it doesn't even feel possible.

When I read about the latest shooting or beheading, my natural response is to dehumanize the people who do these things.

They're monsters. Or demons. And surely Jesus doesn't want me to love monsters or demons. Bad people are one thing, but Satan's BFFs are another.

Except that's not true.

These horrible acts are being committed by people, not monsters. Each one was born. Each one has a mother and a father. They eat. They drink. They breathe. Their hearts beat.

They're human, and, if I take the narrative of the Bible to be true, they're fellow creations of God. They're my brothers and sisters, and they're loved by God.

---

2   But, for real, in the age of cellphones, why does this still happen?

I want to be very clear: I'm not condoning terrorism or mass shootings. I'm also not suggesting we fail to apply legal consequences for those actions.

But if I hate the people who do monstrous things, I'm not hating monsters or demons. I'm hating fellow humans. And I'm refusing to listen to Jesus.

We like to live in a binary, black and white world. A world of "good guys" and "bad guys." But life isn't so cut and dried. Someone can be guilty of terrible things and still merit compassion.

Some "bad guys" suffer from mental illness, personal anguish, or religious manipulation. In the midst of grief for those who suffer, is it possible to spare some compassion for those who've not yet experienced the grace and hope Jesus offers us all?

I'm not seeking to humanize terrorists and murderers because they deserve it or because I'm ignoring their actions. I'm seeking to humanize them because it's true: They're human. They're children of God. They're not beyond redemption.

Taking Jesus seriously is also the only way we can hope to stem the tide of terrorism and shootings at schools, malls, workplaces, and houses of worship. If those atrocities are the work of monsters and demons, I'm powerless to stop them. I can only shake my head and feel sad that monsters and demons can't be stopped.

But if I'm dealing with humans, there's hope. Hope that messages of love, acceptance, and peace can be heard.

Maybe you've heard about the Truth and Reconciliation Commission (TRC) in post-apartheid South Africa. They had an unreasonable task: Resolve decades of anger and injustice built up while a minority people group (white South Africans) abused their power to oppress a majority people group (black South Africans).

Free elections had placed political power in the hands of the black South Africans. They elected Nelson Mandela as president. Many across the globe expected the new government to lead (or at least turn a blind eye) to a civil war in which black South Africans settled old scores.

Instead, the TRC recognized that many people, on both sides, had suffered greatly. Instead of trying to settle scores, they had a mandate to wipe the board clean.

One of their most powerful tools: They could offer amnesty to criminals who confessed to crimes they had committed.

Incredibly, this tool worked to an amazing degree. Families could stop wondering what became of loved ones because confessions allowed this commission to give them answers. Often painful answers, but answers that provided closure and allowed them to move on with their lives.

This effort had success in part because of a determination to see enemies as *people*—no matter what those enemies had done. Flawed people, yes, but people worthy of a chance to start building where they'd once been tearing down the country.

Without that decision, there was no hope for healing. No room for reconciliation.

When enemies are viewed as targets for revenge because of what they've done, there's no getting past the pain, just getting even.[3]

No wonder Jesus wanted us to get out of the revenge business before telling us to take the next step of replacing revenge with love.

But the question remains: How do you love your enemies?

Consider these two unreasonable answers:

Pray for your enemies.

I won't even try to pretend this is my idea because you read it yourself a few pages back and it was Jesus speaking. Jesus himself set this expectation for his followers: "Pray for those who persecute you."

I'm pretty sure he doesn't mean we pray "please give her what she has coming to her" prayers. Nor do I think he means we need to spend an hour each night asking God to pour out blessings on our enemies.

If you have hate in your heart for somebody, maybe your prayer starts with "God, I hate that person, and I don't want to."

As a character in the movie *Shadowlands* said, "[Prayer] doesn't change God—it changes me."

Praying for your enemy opens you up to the work of the Holy Spirit in your heart.

And your relationship with your enemy shifts from a person-to-person relationship to a relationship that includes God. It's only God's presence that can introduce love where there previously was none, grace where grace had been absent, and mercy where it's undeserved.

Forgive your enemies.

Martin Luther King Jr., writing in *Strength to Love*, posits that forgiveness is the decisive factor in how much you can love your enemy.[4] I fully agree. When Jesus looks at his executioners from the cross and offers forgiveness, can there be any doubt about his love for them?

When relatives of the victims in a South Carolina church shooting offered forgiveness to the young man who murdered their loved ones, could anyone doubt they were taking Jesus' words and example seriously?

Loving your enemy doesn't mean you have to add them to your Christmas list or adopt them as your best friend. It means you forgive them, with the knowledge that God is both merciful and just.

I've had some personal experience in praying for and forgiving someone who made himself my enemy. I mentioned in an earlier chapter that I recently

---

3   There's a book all about this. It's called *No Future Without Forgiveness* by Desmond Tutu. I cannot tell you here how strongly I recommend reading it because I require interpretive dance moves to fully convey my recommendation.

4   King, *Strength to Love*, 45.

found myself in an unexpected job transition. That transition was the result of a person acting in a less-than-honorable manner.

In the span of just a few months, my dream job turned into a nightmare. I was lied to and lied about, and my sole goal became to somehow honor God in the midst of a year-long personal struggle.

I prayed for this person and his family for months, but I'll admit there were some days I didn't mean it as much as on other days.

And then one day, while I was standing in my shower, I realized that I was ready to forgive him. I'd never have suddenly decided on my own to forgive someone who selfishly caused me and my family pain, but there it was. In all my soapy splendor, I was ready.[5]

I was ready because I'd spent time inviting the Holy Spirit into the situation through prayer, and that enabled me to work through hurt and anger in a much healthier manner than I'd normally have chosen for myself.

I wouldn't call this person a friend, but he's no longer an enemy. And I'm no longer tempted to seethe in anger or in danger of sinking into sin by resorting to hate.

To paraphrase Dr. King, we don't get rid of enemies with violence. We get rid of enemies by getting rid of hate.[6]

God's goal for our world isn't to eradicate "bad people." It's to eliminate the things that cause people to behave badly.

When Paul writes in Ephesians 6:12, "For we are not fighting against flesh-and-blood enemies, but against evil rulers and authorities of the unseen world, against mighty powers in this dark world, and against evil spirits in the heavenly places," he's telling us point blank that people aren't our real enemies. If we direct our hate or anger toward them, we're pointing it in the wrong direction.

There's evil in our world, and we're called to oppose it, but we're never permitted to make other people collateral damage.

Loving our enemy starts with a choice: to do our best to let go of hate. To ask God to transform our hearts so we're able to love those who hate us.

This, like most of what Jesus says from the Mount, isn't designed to be easy. It's designed to be healthy and fulfilling. And it's designed to be done through the power of the Holy Spirit, not by our own power. This isn't something that happens because of our willpower or our faking it.

When I see people do terrible things through terrorism, war, or abuse, I ask God to shift my response default setting from hate to compassion. To ask, what would lead someone to do what they did? Shattering the lives of others can't be fulfilling, so they must be more miserable or misguided than I could ever imagine.

---

5   Was that TMI? If it was, I'm sorry. If it helps, imagine that I shower fully clothed. Did that help? No? I made it weirder? Okay...um...I'm not sure...you know what? I'm just going to stop. And maybe go take a shower...

6   King, *Strength to Love.*

That compassion also extends to the victims. I can't stand in my generally comfortable life and think I truly understand the pain of those who suffer because of the actions of others. How well would I handle the loss of my wife or daughters at the hands of a murderer? I can't image how hard it must be to face such a circumstance—and selfishly, I hope I never find out.

Some say that's too great a burden to carry, and they're right—if they attempt to shoulder it alone.

All we can do in response to Jesus' unreasonable expectation is look to him, forgive as we're empowered to do so, grieve for those who suffer, and seek to have compassion for those who cause pain...including pain to us and those we love.

And we can keep this in mind, too: Being faithful to forgive those who wrong us in small ways readies us to forgive when we suffer greater wrongs in the future.

▌▌ A Brief Pause

Loving our enemies: Easy in theory; hard to do when someone's hurting a person you love. But if Jesus is really serious...

Jesus' unreasonable expectations always reveal something about him. What does his insistence that we love our enemies tell you about him?

_____

_____

_____

Where in your life do you struggle with loving those who hurt you in some way? Or isn't that ever a struggle for you?

_____

_____

_____

_____

How willing are you to walk away from your "right" to extract revenge on those who injure you in some way?

_____

_____

_____

_____

Chapter 9

GIVE TO THE NEEDY

Watch out! Don't do your good deeds publicly, to be admired by others, for you will lose the reward from your Father in heaven. When you give to someone in need, don't do as the hypocrites do— blowing trumpets in the synagogues and streets to call attention to their acts of charity! I tell you the truth, they have received all the reward they will ever get. But when you give to someone in need, don't let your left hand know what your right hand is doing. Give your gifts in private, and your Father, who sees everything, will reward you.

—Matthew 6:1-4

We've been challenged by Jesus not to hate those who hate us.

Now Jesus moves on in his sermon—but he doesn't move far.[1]

This portion of the Sermon on the Mount is often trotted out as a caution to not showboat—to not insist on recognition for good deeds. And that message is certainly there in Jesus' words.

But I believe Jesus is getting at something deeper as well.

I believe Jesus is challenging us not to harm those we're trying to help.

Here's why I say that: Jesus is obviously annoyed that certain people expect to be admired when they do something for others. These people aren't as

---

1 If I had been at the Sermon, I think by this point I would have moved from shocked silence to breathing into whatever the first-century equivalent of a paper bag was.

interested in providing help as in polishing up their reputations and creating an appearance of generosity.

Jesus' comments point to a truth in God's Kingdom: True generosity isn't just reflected in making a donation. Of greater importance is having a faithful, healthy heart when you give.

Do this for me: Imagine that some calamity has fallen on you and your family. You're shocked to discover all your money is gone, and you can't even afford shelter, much less food and clothing for you and your loved ones.

You need help, so you turn to people in a faith community for that help. They're willing to assist you, but first you have to do a few things.

You have to take a selfie with the person providing assistance—and that photo will be posted to your benefactor's social media network. Tons of people who live in your town will see it and know you received charity.

Next, you have to film a video explaining how helpless you are and that you'll never make it without the faith community that's helping you. They'll screen this video at the start of all their church services from now on.

Finally, all the clothes they give you have been marked with a huge patch indicating that you got them through charity.

Here's why all that is so distasteful: It robs charity recipients of their dignity. The point of the charity in the scenario I just described is clearly not to help you and your family but to make the giver look better. Your desperate need has been used for the givers' own personal fulfillment.

In the book *Toxic Charity*, author Robert Lupton makes the case that when we help others from a misguided place of wanting to make ourselves look superior, or to assuage our guilt, we end up hurting those to whom we're offering help. Specifically, Lupton says that when we assist people, we need to make sure we're giving them dignity and helping strengthen their support network even as we encourage them regarding their work ethic and entrepreneurship.[2]

To truly give a hand up rather than a hand out, as the saying goes.

Am I reading too much into what Jesus said in his sermon? I don't think so.

Everything Jesus said and did—here and elsewhere—is motivated by love. And if he's warning us to not cut ourselves off from God's blessings by insisting on public recognition, that's a loving caution.

He's urging us to not shortchange ourselves by giving up eternal blessings for short-term popularity.

And if he's lovingly caring for the givers, why wouldn't he also lovingly care for those receiving charity? After all, he loves them, too.

I suspect that's one reason Jesus sets an unreasonable expectation for those who do good: Do good, but not for applause. Do good for the right reasons.

---

2   Robert D. Lupton, *Toxic Charity* (New York, HarperCollins, 2011), 130.

The notion of respecting the dignity of others is an important concept tucked into a small, not-well-known book of the New Testament: the book of Philemon.[3]

The Apostle Paul sends a runaway slave (Onesimus) who has become a believer back to his master (Philemon)—a master who's already a believer. Along with the letter, Paul sends an expectation that Philemon won't punish Onesimus, especially since Onesimus has been assisting Paul.

Reading between the lines, Paul is asking Philemon to grant Onesimus his freedom.

Yet Paul doesn't simply say, "As God's apostle, you're going to do what I tell you." Instead, Paul asks the owner to treat Onesimus the same way Philemon would treat Paul.[4]

In *Paul and the Faithfulness of God*, author N.T. Wright makes the case that if Paul has to wrestle a begrudging willingness to be kind from a believer in a position of power to assist a believer who's vulnerable, it's a failure in the eyes of the Gospel.[5]

This is because the Gospel, as Paul writes elsewhere, makes us all truly equal: "There is no longer Jew or Gentile, slave or free, male and female. For you are all one in Christ Jesus" (Galatians 3:28).

Paul's not saying that Christians become genderless, cultureless, purposeless automatons. Rather, he's saying that our identity in Jesus cuts across all other identities, creating unity where there's been division.

Not conformity, but rather unity in the midst of diversity.

Sure, we're different—but when we stand before God we have equal value, which is our basis for relating to one another.

In the midst of this, Paul has a tricky social issue with which to contend. Yes, Philemon and Onesimus are equals before God, but one is a slave and one a slave owner. The social structure stands at odds with the Kingdom reality of equality.[6]

Paul chooses to not play the apostle card with Philemon because doing so is the exact opposite approach to what Paul is asking Philemon to take with Onesimus. Paul is modeling for Philemon how it feels to be treated as an equal in the hopes that Philemon will also treat Onesimus as an equal.

---

3   Don't feel bad if you had to Google "Philemon" to make sure I wasn't making this up. It doesn't even have any chapters because it's only 25 verses long. To get there, pass the Gospels and Acts, and then skip over the long letters Paul wrote. When you get to Timothy, start slowing down. It's after Titus. If you hit Hebrews, you went too far.

4   Philemon 1:17

5   Nicholas Thomas Wright, *Paul and the Faithfulness of God* (Minneapolis, Augsburg Fortress, 2013).

6   By the way, in case you're horrified that Paul isn't simply telling Philemon how evil slavery is and to knock it off, keep in mind that slavery back then, while not exactly a good thing, was much different from the chattel slavery of early America.

If apostle, master, and slave can all exist in community, the body of Christ is working. In that world, in that time, such a community was completely unreasonable—and exactly what Jesus had in mind.

Equally unreasonable is Jesus' value that those who help are to give assistance not from a lofty place of superiority but from a grateful recognition that they've been helped as well. Rescued even, courtesy of Jesus.

With that in mind, here are some thoughts about giving that's inclusive and healthy:

Be humble.

James, the brother of Jesus and leader of the church in Jerusalem, wrote this: "Believers who are poor have something to boast about, for God has honored them. And those who are rich should boast that God has humbled them. They will fade away like a little flower in the field" (James 1:9-10).

We often encounter the upside-down economy of the Kingdom of God.

If you want to be first, make yourself last.

When you give, you'll get.

Pray for your enemies. Pray for people who hurt you.

When someone wrongs you, forgive them.[7]

So we shouldn't be surprised when James tells us that being rich and poor work differently in the Kingdom of God.

Prior to Jesus' time on earth, the common assumption was that if God was pleased with you, you'd be well off. Indeed, Job's friends all believed Job must have sinned greatly for so much tragedy to fall on him and his family. Here's a sample of what his friends said to him:

"[The riches of the wicked] will not last, and their wealth will not endure. Their possessions will no longer spread across the horizon" (Job15:29).

In other words, you must have done *something* to deserve this. You did something wrong, and that's why you're experiencing financial calamity.

Yet the Apostle James rewrote the equation. James contended that being poor might actually be a blessing from God.

This obviously conflicts greatly with The American Dream, and that's a challenge for American believers. It's also a reminder: We need to bring our cultural perspectives in line with the Gospel rather than trying to shape the Gospel to fit our preferences and comfort zones.

Which means instead of viewing people who need help as inferior, we can count it a privilege to be a blessing to a brother or sister who needs us. After all, in the Kingdom we're all children of the same Father.

Have compassion, not pity.

Pity says, "You're down there, I'm up here, and that makes me sad." Compassion, however, revises that statement. It says, "We're equals, and we'll face these challenges together."

---

7   Luke 14:11; Luke 6:38; Matthew 5:44; and Matthew 18:22 respectively

Arrogance leads to pity. Humility leads to compassion.

Pity maintains the divisions that exist in our world, while compassion tears them down.

Pity would have led Jesus to merely be sad we were perishing as a consequence of our own choices. Instead, his compassion led to the redemption of humanity. He did nothing to deserve living in a broken and fallen world, but he joined us in it anyway. And today he welcomes us in to be part of his process of renewing all Creation.

When you see a person living homeless on the streets or learn about children dying from war, famine, or disease; when you encounter a person who lost her faith after suffering abuse or tragedy—refuse to offer pity.

Instead, be like Jesus and bring compassion.

Make giving money your last resort.

In *Toxic Charity*, Lupton says that if we only ever give money to people in need, we end up doing more harm than good, despite our intentions:

"give once and you elicit appreciation;
give twice and you create anticipation;
give three times and you create expectation;
give four times and it becomes entitlement;
give five times and you establish dependency."[8]

For several years I've volunteered with the Salvation Army in downtown Baltimore. I'll take one or more of my kids along as we prepare meals and ride around town to distribute those meals on what's called the Feedmore Truck.

The driver is a Salvation Army employee named Mr. Luther. At the stops, while volunteers stay in the truck distributing food through a side window, Mr. Luther stands outside to manage the line and interact with people.

I only see Mr. Luther get mad for two reasons: When people leave trash lying around after eating, and when someone asks what food is being offered before deciding whether he or she wants it.

Mr. Luther will pointedly say, "It's a meal. Do you want it or not?"

I'm glad my kids and I are part of an effort to feed the hungry, but Lupton would maintain that's just the beginning of offering *real* help.

Lupton says that to keep from accidentally creating dependency through charity, we need to intentionally create empowerment by investing in the lives of people we're helping. This requires taking time to discover talents and abilities and to uncover resources that can be developed.

In other words, it's much more than simply dropping some change into a cup or sliding a brown bag through a truck window.

This echoes what Martin Luther King Jr. had to say about charity: "The hardhearted person lacks the capacity for genuine compassion...He gives dollars to a worthwhile charity, but he gives not of his spirit."[9]

---

8   Lupton, *Toxic Charity*, 130.
9   King, *Strength to Love*, 6.

Please don't misunderstand what I'm saying. Giving money is an important part of charity, but it's by no means the *only* part of charity.

No nonprofit is going to tell you to just keep your money; they all know they can put the dollars to good use.

But when you offer to donate your time, talent, and concern—that's what changes lives. And that's what leads to "good deeds" that aren't easily observable.

Few people will see you visit the school to mentor an at-risk kid.

Or pick up the phone to connect with and encourage a grieving widow.

Or write to a prisoner to let him know he's not been forgotten.

I know of a lady who contacted World Vision—an organization that lets you sponsor at-need children across the world. The woman said she couldn't afford to sponsor any more children, but she had time to write letters to kids who didn't get communication from their actual sponsors. They gave her a list of kids to start writing to, and she did it with great enthusiasm. She certainly gave of her spirit.

Giving money is good, but there's opportunity for so much more. And, as Jesus pointed out, material giving can easily become about the giver, not the recipient.

A question: How are you giving of yourself to those who are in need?

Perhaps you volunteer time on a regular basis. Or you look for opportunities to talk with people who are often overlooked, people who don't often have friendly, respectful conversations.

Perhaps you set aside time to pray for people who you know are in need.

Money may represent your time and energy (you had to earn it, right?), but it's not a substitute for your personal presence in the lives of others. Money can do many things, but it can't create community with other people.[10]

Be interruptible.

My friend Drew felt challenged by God one day to say hello to a man he'd passed by for years at a Washington, D.C. metro stop. The man didn't actively ask for money; he simply stood at the top of the escalator and wished everyone a good morning. He held a cup for those who wanted to give him money. The man also happened to be blind.

So on this one particular morning, Drew stepped out of the rush of humanity squeezing down an escalator to say hello to this man.

Drew introduced himself, and it led to a conversation that deeply impacted my friend. He learned the man's name was John. Drew discovered that John wasn't born blind but was blinded in an accident when John was 40 years old.

And Drew found that John was also a follower of Jesus—one who took great joy in wishing everyone who rushed past him a good morning so that, perhaps, their days might start off in a positive way.

---

10   To my fellow introverts: I know part of you is cringing over this thought. Please
     don't push this challenge away.

This encounter made a difference in Drew's life. He'd paused one busy morning hoping to somehow be a blessing to this man and, in the end, gained a new friendship.

Drew gave of himself rather than just dropping some money in a cup and calling it a good deed.

The Holy Spirit had tapped Drew on the shoulder, and Drew was willing to be interrupted to obey what God told him to do.[11]

One of the things I like best about Jesus is that he's always willing to be interrupted.

A woman suffering a health issue interrupts Jesus as Jesus is hurrying off to meet with an important community leader. Jesus pauses, stopping long enough to be sure her healing is not only physical but spiritual and emotional as well.[12]

At another point in his ministry, Jesus wants to escape the crush of the crowds and heads off in a boat—but people anticipate where he'll land and run ahead. When Jesus and his disciples pull ashore, a huge crowd is waiting. Rather than getting angry or setting off again, Jesus has compassion on the crowd and begins to teach them.[13]

When a Roman Centurion, a hated member of an oppressive government, asks Jesus to heal his servant, Jesus is willing to drop everything and go to his house.[14]

In each of these situations, Jesus values people more than his preferences or agenda. No one is too insignificant to be valued when they encounter Jesus.

While I'd love to live in a world where no one has needs, the reality is that we can't fix inequity or injustice. Even Jesus says we'll always have poverty in our world.[15]

These issues *will* be solved in the age to come, when the Kingdom of God fully arrives. But for now, the neediness around us is an opportunity for us to love people in the midst of this world's brokenness.

Maybe we can't solve poverty, but we can give as Jesus urged his audience to give—with genuine humility and love.

---

11 It is humbling to me that he was reading my Lent devotional, *A Reason to Hope*, when he was inspired to take this action.

12 Luke 8:43-48

13 See Mark 6:30-34. But seriously, if crowds of desperate people followed me around everywhere I went nonstop, the over/under for when I'd snap is 48 hours. Jesus did this for somewhere between one and three years and continued to have compassion. If that's all I knew about Jesus, I'd already be willing to listen to anything he said.

14 Matthew 8:5-13

15 Matthew 26:11

▌▌ A Brief Pause

It's not enough for Jesus that we give—we have to give for the *right reasons*, too. Once more Jesus blows straight past our actions to focus on our hearts...

Given what Jesus says about giving, how does your giving stack up? And how do you feel about that?

_____

_____

_____

Describe a time someone gave to you in the respectful manner Jesus describes. What was the gift, and how did it strike you at the time?

_____

_____

_____

What do Jesus' words reveal about his heart concerning giving...and those who need help?

_____

_____

_____

_____

Chapter 10
PRAYER

When you pray, don't be like the hypocrites who love to pray publicly on street corners and in the synagogues where everyone can see them. I tell you the truth, that is all the reward they will ever get. But when you pray, go away by yourself, shut the door behind you, and pray to your Father in private. Then your Father, who sees everything, will reward you.

When you pray, don't babble on and on as the Gentiles do. They think their prayers are answered merely by repeating their words again and again. Don't be like them, for your Father knows exactly what you need even before you ask him! Pray like this:

Our Father in heaven, may your name be kept holy.

May your Kingdom come soon.

May your will be done on earth, as it is in heaven.

Give us today the food we need, and forgive us our sins, as we have forgiven those who sin against us.

And don't let us yield to temptation,
but rescue us from the evil one.

If you forgive those who sin against you,
your heavenly Father will forgive you.
But if you refuse to forgive others, your
Father will not forgive your sins.

And when you fast, don't make it obvious, as
the hypocrites do, for they try to look miserable
and disheveled so people will admire them for
their fasting. I tell you the truth, that is the only
reward they will ever get. But when you fast, comb
your hair and wash your face. Then no one will
notice that you are fasting, except your Father,
who knows what you do in private. And your
Father, who sees everything, will reward you.

—*Matthew 6:5-18*

One of my hobbies is trying to manipulate God.

I don't think it's a particularly healthy hobby, and it's certainly not a productive one, but what can I say? I'm self-centered, and like a car that pulls to one side, I often find myself drifting over the line into manipulative behavior.

At least that's what I do when I'm not fully living the emotionally and relationally healthy life Jesus calls me to live. Put simply: I just want things to go according to my plans and desires.

One of my favorite tactics is to offer God a "horse trade" deal. You know, "God, if you'll do X for me, I'll do Y for you."

My goal in these deals is to make what I'm offering so helpful, so useful to God that God would be crazy to say no. And since God isn't crazy, it's basically a foolproof plan.

To steal a line from *The Godfather*, I make God an offer he can't refuse.

Yet this never seems to work. Good thing, too, because if God gave in, it would indicate that God doesn't have much of a plan.

And if *that's* the case, we're all in deep trouble.

Prayer, as Jesus models it in his sermon, helps me break away from my self-centeredness and be fully oriented toward God. To pray as Jesus prayed is to embrace the reality that what God really wants is to connect with me—intimately.

There's nothing unusual about a rabbi like Jesus teaching about prayer. Rabbis prayed often and encouraged others to do the same. Notice Jesus said, "*When* you pray," not "*If* you pray."

But what certainly struck his listeners as unusual—and likely unreasonable—was Jesus' intimate tone with God.

The Jews of Jesus' time were accustomed to thinking of God as the Father of their nation but not necessarily as a personal father. It's the difference between thinking of your father as a somewhat distant and starched patriarch and thinking of him as your daddy.

The first carries great respect, but the second is a much closer personal connection.

Too often we've turned Jesus' model prayer into a recipe and missed the point: We can have an intimate relationship with the God of the universe who's willing to let us waltz into his throne room anytime, without an appointment, for a chat.

That's the unreasonable idea on display in this prayer.

But that it's unreasonable doesn't mean it's not true.

While Jesus' prayer isn't a recipe, let's take a closer look at it line by line. We'll find some incredible truths he packed into such a small number of words.

"Our"
Who am I?

In chapter 3, I made my case that the purpose of our existence is "community." That God is community and we were created to share in community with God.

Jesus using the word *our* rather than *my* is a reminder that we're in community and not just doing life with God alone. We're also in community with everyone else who enters that God-community. We're not alone. We have many, many brothers and sisters, and God loves all of us.

Who are we? In addition to whoever we are as individuals, we're part of a community.

"Father"
Who are you?

We're not praying to a butler who lives to fulfill our every wish.

We're not praying to a dictator who does what he wants no matter what.

We're praying to the God who created us, the Father who knows everything about us. Who knows everything we've said, thought, and done…yet still loves us.

My experience as the father of three beautiful, crazy, smart, creative, crazy, fun, crazy kids has taught me a lot about how father relationships are supposed to work.[1]

---

1   I mentioned crazy, right?

A father protects you but also gives you the freedom to make choices and learn from those choices.

A father is proud of you when you've given it your all and will help you when you've bitten off more than you can chew.

Sometimes a father has to help you discover what you're capable of.

Before my son was old enough to tag along, I took my two daughters for a night of camping at the beach. The beach is about three hours away from our house, so it was dark when we arrived. It also just so happened there were gale force winds in the area when we showed up.[2]

As we struggled to set up our tent in the dark, wind whipped sand against us so fiercely that it felt like we were being pelted by tiny bullets.

My daughters both began screaming in pain and terror as I assured them that "We're having an adventure!" and that "This will make a great story one day!"[3] Fortunately, their screaming didn't affect the other campers because there weren't any. Literally. Every other campsite was empty.

Eventually, we moved to a campsite farther from the shore, one protected by small hedges so I could actually assemble our tent.

My daughters speak of that trip as a legendary disaster (we did eventually have to pack up and leave at 2:00 a.m. when the tent started flooding), but they discovered they could endure a chaotic and challenging situation.

Had they been in real danger, I'd have quickly gotten them out of there. Instead, I let them face a bit of adversity so they could grow stronger knowing they'd faced it.

We're praying to a Father who wants the best for us. And sometimes what's best comes through challenges we'd rather not face.

"in heaven"
Where are you, God...and where am I?

It's a mind-bender for me to think of God being off somewhere in heaven yet also living in our hearts. But that thought falls into place if you picture heaven not as a place far off in outer space but rather as a different reality that exists all around us.

I'd even argue that heaven is more real than anything you're sensing around you right now.

Prayer is one way we connect with God, who's heaven personified. When we pray, we're relating with God who is, as Anne Lamott says in *Help, Thanks, Wow*, both way beyond us and deep inside us.[4]

And not only is heaven everywhere, but it exists in the past, present, and future at the same time. One reason Jesus sometimes seems less urgently

---

2   Checking the weather before setting out is for the birds. Intelligent, well-prepared birds.

3   Classic dad move, by the way: pretending there's something good about a situation that has gone completely awry.

4   Anne Lamott, *Help, Thanks, Wow* (New York, Riverhead Books, 2012).

concerned with our crisis of the moment[5] than we are is because he knows that God has already created a future in which he fulfills the promises he has made—including redemption and salvation for all who trust him.

"may your name be kept holy"
It's a good idea for me to remember who I'm talking to.

I could wax eloquently about how prayer is more than tossing wish lists at God and trying to get him to deliver, but I've already confessed I'm a Serial Prayer Manipulator, so my credibility is shot.

But let me say this: Jesus clearly doesn't see prayer being solely about our concerns. Rather, it's also an opportunity to remember what's important to God.

One of those things? God cares—a lot—about his name being holy. About it being honored. Revered. Held in high esteem.

And since God is inviting me into relationship, this is an opportunity for me to care about what matters to him.

None of us is in the market for a friend who only remembers our phone number when it's moving day, right? So when we get to the part where I'm sharing my very real needs with God, it's important that I keep in mind that I have the Creator of the universe on the other end of the line, and there are things he wants to talk about as well.

"May your Kingdom come soon. May your will be done on earth, as it is in heaven."
Why are we here?

Our highest calling in life isn't to skate on through problem free. It's to engage the world in such a way that the purposes of the Kingdom of God are advanced. To invite the Kingdom of God into our lives and let it impact the world around us.

Jesus tosses out a *hugely* unreasonable expectation here: That no matter what we pray, we keep the big picture in mind. We've been given a mission of cooperating with God's purposes, and everything—including our prayers— needs to align with God's will. And not necessarily with our own.

Do your prayers normally reflect that you're first and foremost committed to doing God's will? to sharing the God community with everyone you encounter? to speaking justice in the world? to laying down your life for others?

It's a tall order, but quite simply, it's exactly what we see Jesus do.

Jesus' prayer brings our calling—following in his footsteps—into sharp focus.

---

5   See Matthew 8:23-27 when the disciples are freaking out over a storm threatening to sink them—and remember, many of them are fishermen so they know sailing— only to find Jesus sleeping in the boat.

"Give us today the food we need"

Where's what I need?

Funny how long we have to go before we reach the part where Jesus teaches us it's okay to ask for stuff. My prayers all too often jump straight here.

It's good to know that God *does* care about what we need and that Jesus wants us to talk about our needs with God.

But notice that Jesus models our praying for true needs rather than wants.

I *want* more money and a bigger house, but perhaps I *need* to recognize that I have clothes to wear, food to eat, and a roof over my head.

I *want* guidance about what to do next in life, but I *need* to be grateful for the gift of salvation that's changing my life.

Jesus' simple request is a reminder for us to place our faith in God. To trust him to provide what we really need in life. Frankly, it would be very difficult—perhaps impossible—to have that trust had we not first dealt with the issues Jesus raises earlier in his prayer.

And Jesus goes on to zero in on something we *truly* need: to forgive and be forgiven.

"and forgive us our sins, as we have forgiven those who sin against us"

This isn't about just me or just you; it's about us.

Jesus doesn't let us walk away from this prayer dusting off our hands, proclaiming in a self-satisfied way that it's all in his hands and there's nothing further for us to do. We *always* have further opportunity for engagement.

As Martin Luther King Jr. wrote, "Prayer is a marvelous and necessary supplement of our feeble efforts, but it is a dangerous substitute."[6]

Clearly, prayer is important. It's integral—*necessary*—but it's not an opportunity to fill God's to-do list while we sit back and twiddle our thumbs. Prayer is part of a relationship we've been invited to participate in, a relationship in which God tends to work in us and through us rather than completely separate from us.

And here in his prayer, Jesus gives us one more upside-down heavenly economic principle: The way to get more grace is to give more away.

Immediately after this prayer, Jesus goes on to drop a bomb: God will treat us the way we treat others. I don't know about you, but this terrifies me. I'm a selfish person, often seeking my own comfort and convenience. Some days the best I can do is ignore others; other days I manage to inconvenience them in pursuit of benefiting myself.

But here's the good news: As I grow in my ability to forgive and to freely give grace, I'm ultimately benefiting myself. There's no need for me to worry about being used by others when my generosity isn't appreciated or is taken

---

6   King, *Strength to Love*, 138.

advantage of. Why? Because I'm essentially making a deposit into my own personal bank account of grace.

"And don't let us yield to temptation, but rescue us from the evil one"

We need rescuing.

In this final line of his prayer, Jesus reaffirms that we depend on God's grace. It's a simple idea, though one we sometimes seem to actively ignore.

Like it or not, we rely on the God who walked this earth for grace, for love, for life itself. We need rescuing. As much as we wish we were self-sufficient, we're not.

And maybe that's the biggest reason to not pray mindlessly but rather to fully engage with God: *We need rescuing.* From sin. From temptation. From evil.

Thank God he's not only willing but also wanting to rescue us.

Because he's not just all-powerful…he's our loving Father.

Jesus' model prayer is shockingly short. On several occasions, the Gospels describe Jesus going off and spending an extended period of time in prayer.[7] So why are we given such a small snippet?

I wish I had an answer to that question. No records exist of what Jesus said or did in most of those situations.

Here's what we *do* know: Simple, genuine words matter more than eloquent, polished-up-for-presentation prayers. Jesus isn't teaching people to *look* more spiritual; he's teaching us to *be* more spiritual.

I'm sure you know the difference between the two. No? Allow me to illustrate.

The first time I accompanied my wife (at the time, my fiancée) back home to meet her family, I got a chance to meet her grandfather. This man had been a pioneer missionary who traveled deep into South American jungles to tell tribes about Jesus Christ. He was a deeply spiritual man who kept a prayer list that took him hours to pray through daily.

When we gathered at the table for dinner, I expected his prayer of thanksgiving for the meal might go just a wee bit longer than my typical prayer in the same situation.

I wasn't wrong.

He genuinely and sincerely gave thanks and spoke to God with an easy familiarity with the God he loved.

---

7   Matthew 14:23 and Luke 6:12 recall two such instances. We can also safely presume Jesus spent extended time praying while in the wilderness after his baptism. Surely there were more of these instances; these happen to be moments captured by the Gospel writers.

When the prayer was over, I had tears in my eyes. I'm sure I looked supremely spiritual to everyone at the table in that moment, brought to tears by such a simple and elegant time of devotion.

Let me tell you what *actually* happened.

While Grandpa was praying, I arranged my hands into the holiest-looking manner possible: flat hands pressed against one another directly in front of my face. Remember, I needed this guy to like me so I could marry his granddaughter.

During the prayer, I happened to notice that a hair was sticking out of my nose and touching my fingertips. Since everyone had their eyes closed, I decided I could take care of this grooming need during the prayer time. I pinched the hair and gave it a hard tug.

The English language cannot adequately express the pain I felt as that hair refused to budge.

My eyes immediately began to water from the pain.

I managed to stay silent as the prayer continued, but when Grandpa said "amen," I looked up, tears filling my eyes, and excused myself to the bathroom.

Though everyone else at that table probably thought I was spiritual, you now know better. What appeared spiritual really wasn't.[8]

In an excellent talk at TEDxBaltimore a few years ago, Molly McGrath Tierney spoke about the danger of any organization or person becoming really good at doing the wrong things.[9]

In the church, in spite of Jesus' cautions, I fear sometimes we have become really good at *looking* spiritual instead of *being* spiritual.

Now I'm not criticizing the use of memorized prayer or a resource such as the *Book of Common Prayer*. I'm simply saying that they don't replace honest and open expression to God in prayer that flows straight from our hearts.

When I read the psalms, I see David and the other writers of the songs being incredibly open with difficult emotions or even frustration with God.

The author of Psalm 44 writes, "Wake up, O Lord! Why do you sleep? Get up! Do not reject us forever. Why do you look the other way? Why do you ignore our suffering and oppression? We collapse in the dust, lying face down in the dirt. Rise up! Help us! Ransom us because of your unfailing love."

In Psalm 3, David prays "Arise, O Lord! Rescue me, my God! Slap all my enemies in the face! Shatter the teeth of the wicked!"

Imagine if I got up on stage at my church, asked everyone to bow their heads for prayer, and then said any of those things. People would be shocked. Offended.

---

8   If you don't like TMI, get away from this footnote right now, because I'm going to tell you what happened in the bathroom. I found a pair of tweezers and pulled that sucker out. It wasn't one hair. It was three that had somehow fused/braided together. Pulling it out was in the top 5 painful experiences of my life. I've never had anything like that happen again. Freak nose hair incident.

9   https://www.youtube.com/watch?v=c15hy8dXSps

Yet despite his failings, David was called a man after God's own heart in part because he openly shared his emotions with God and invited God's response. When David asked God to destroy his enemies, it makes me uncomfortable because violent texts don't fit well with my concept of God being a loving Father.

But I don't have to assume that God actually endorsed David's prayer. God simply allowed David to express rage or depression in the situations David faced. And David trusted God with his real feelings, knowing that God loved him even in the midst of his despair, fear, and anger.

Just like God loves us—you and me—in the midst of our despair, fear, and anger. Or our joy. Or whatever else we're feeling.

Once I realized God isn't afraid of my feelings or upset by them, I began opening up more to God. And I found that opening myself up let me invite God into those places to bring healing.

It's not that being open and authentic means God will necessarily "fix" what's vexing me. Rather, it creates space for him to bring healing and comfort.

God's not looking for people who can pray the prettiest prayers. He's looking for the ones courageous enough to take off their masks and be themselves, trusting that God's love is bigger than their hurts and concern about appearing perfect in front of others.

Here are a few lessons I've learned about how my prayers—and yours—can echo the intimacy and authenticity of Jesus' model prayer:

Seek to be open and authentic.

God doesn't need me to be forthcoming because he wonders what I'm really thinking and feeling. God already knows. When God called out to Adam and Eve in the Garden of Eden, "Where are you?" (Genesis 3:9), it wasn't because God is terrible at playing hide-and-seek. God knew where Adam was. He wanted *Adam* to understand where Adam was—separated from God.

When I was going through a particularly difficult time in my life, I actually started my prayer time every morning by saying, "God I feel _____ today." Some days the fill-in-the-blank was "angry." Other days it was "optimistic," "frustrated," "confused," "scared," or "hopeful."

I didn't do this because God needed the information. I did it because I knew I could trust God with my feelings and because until I knew where I was, I wouldn't know how to connect with God in a genuine way.

Don't worry about using the "right words."

Understand that prayer is about being transformed by God, not finding the magic words that prompt him to do what you want.

God's not a genie waiting to hear the magic words that force him to take action,[10] and he's not interested in trading favors and deals.

Loving fathers don't worry about hearing all the right words—they look at the heart *behind* the words.

And God is a loving Father.

A Father who's more concerned with who you are than with the words you use.

While we're desperately trying to get God to fix what's uncomfortable in our lives, God's often asking us to engage with the very circumstances and the people who make us uncomfortable.

When David wrote in Psalm 23:4, "Even when I walk through the darkest valley, I will not be afraid, for you are close beside me," notice he didn't say, "*If* I ever walk though such a valley, I'm sure you'd be there."

It wasn't a theoretical situation for David, who'd walked many dark valleys and been a hair's breadth away from death many times. He knew God wouldn't abandon him in those moments, because he'd been in the valley and seen God's faithfulness in those moments.

There are many times in the Psalms where David begs God to change his circumstances. But David clearly understood that even when nothing seemed to change, God was still with him.

Believing God was leading the way, my wife and I bought a business several years ago. We bought the business just as the economy headed into the dumpster, and our company rapidly ate through our hard-earned savings.

I tried to find the right words to convince God to save our business. To do something. To do *anything*. But the business collapsed, leaving our finances in tatters, as well as leaving us frustrated with God.

In time I began hearing what God was saying to me about our business failure. I still don't have all the answers, but it was when I was praying that I was reminded God was with us—even in failure.

Even in the valley.

Make prayer a part of your life, not a compartment of it.

The Apostle Paul told one of the churches under his care that they should "never stop praying"(1 Thessalonians 5:17).

Paul assumed that prayer was an integral part of life, that believers will find their hearts and minds regularly, perhaps constantly, turning toward God.

That's Jesus' assumption too.

When it comes to Jesus' expectation that prayer be something that's an ongoing attitude in my life, I think about a toaster.

---

10   By the way, if you ever encounter a genie, make sure your first wish is for more wishes. When the genie says you can't do that, make your second wish that you CAN do that. (drops microphone)

A toaster's function is to make toast,[11] and I happen to like toast. So let's say I buy a toaster and bring it home from the store. And this isn't just any old toaster; it's a *nice* expensive one with a brushed chrome finish, multiple browning settings, and LED indicator lights.

I pull it out of the box, slide a couple of slices of bread into the slots, and push down the lever. I busy myself pulling together jam, butter, and a knife.

But after several minutes, let's also say that nothing is happening. No heat. No comforting smell of warm toast. No LED lights flashing on.

Therefore, no toast.

A quick inspection reveals that I failed to plug in the toaster, something I can quickly remedy to get the whole toast experience back on track.

My point: I may have the best possible toaster, one designed to make the most fantastically delicious toast ever, but without being connected to the electric grid, it won't fulfill its purpose in life.

When I'm not making prayer a regular part of my life, I'm like that unplugged toaster. I can't have the healthy, fulfilling, complete life God designed for me if I'm not connected to him.

It feels unreasonable that God is inviting me to share my angriest, most selfish, most insecure thoughts with him, but that's exactly what Jesus says to do.

In fact, given what Jesus says, it's the *only* way to pray.

Jesus has changed the rules yet again. Gone is the need to be concerned about crafting carefully worded prayers. He's inviting us to instead do as he does: to speak with a Father who loves him, who wants to know what he thinks and feels.

And praying to impress others who might be watching? Complete waste of time. That's a currency that can't be spent; what others think isn't important.

Only what God thinks.

The God who counts it as joy to have us open ourselves up with reckless abandon before him, to come to him with all we are and all that's in us.

That sort of prayer is freeing…and terrifying. And exactly what Jesus calls us to experience.

---

11   Stop me if I'm going too fast here.

▐▐ A Brief Pause

Jesus models an authentic conversation with God, one that gets past formulas to transparency. And he's suggesting that we do the same.

If someone were to listen in to your prayers, would those prayers be described as formulaic...or authentic? What do you think has shaped how you pray?

_____

_____

_____

Jesus lets us listen in to a conversation between the Son and the Father. What did you discover about each from what you overheard?

_____

_____

_____

_____

I mentioned that it's easier to look spiritual than to be spiritual. Assuming you've fallen into this trap a time or two (I _thought_ you looked familiar), describe how it happened...and why.

_____

_____

_____

_____

Chapter 11
MONEY AND POSSESSIONS

Don't store up treasures here on earth, where moths eat them and rust destroys them, and where thieves break in and steal. Store your treasures in heaven, where moths and rust cannot destroy, and thieves do not break in and steal. Wherever your treasure is, there the desires of your heart will also be.

Your eye is like a lamp that provides light for your body. When your eye is healthy, your whole body is filled with light. But when your eye is unhealthy, your whole body is filled with darkness. And if the light you think you have is actually darkness, how deep that darkness is!

No one can serve two masters. For you will hate one and love the other; you will be devoted to one and despise the other. You cannot serve God and be enslaved to money.

That is why I tell you not to worry about everyday life—whether you have enough food and drink, or enough clothes to wear. Isn't life more than food, and your body more than clothing? Look at the birds. They don't plant or harvest or store food in barns, for your heavenly Father feeds them. And aren't you far more valuable to him than they are? Can all your worries add a single moment to your life?

And why worry about your clothing? Look at the lilies of the field and how they grow. They don't work or make their clothing, yet Solomon in all his glory was not dressed as beautifully as they are. And if God cares so wonderfully for wildflowers that are here today and thrown into the fire tomorrow, he will certainly care for you. Why do you have so little faith?

So don't worry about these things, saying, "What will we eat? What will we drink? What will we wear?" These things dominate the thoughts of unbelievers, but your heavenly Father already knows all your needs. Seek the Kingdom of God above all else, and live righteously, and he will give you everything you need.

So don't worry about tomorrow, for tomorrow will bring its own worries. Today's trouble is enough for today.

—Matthew 6:19-34

So now, added to the list of unreasonable expectations Jesus is handing out in the Sermon on the Mount (such as "don't hate" and "don't lust"), we can toss in "don't worry."

Specifically, don't worry about money.

Um…right.

That Jesus makes a direct connection between how his audience views money and the presence of worry in their lives shows he knows them. And us.

Let's consider his comments about money and then ask how his challenge not to worry about it can impact other areas of our lives as well.

It's not all about the Benjamins.

Not all that long ago the United States had the largest lottery jackpot in history—over $1.5 billion.

People went bonkers, many of them spending a considerable amount of money in search of a winning ticket.

I know some people will have a problem with this, but I bought a ticket.[1] I never for a minute thought I'd actually win.[2] The reason I bought the ticket was so my family could enjoy the entertainment of "what would we do with it" conversations.

I'm not disappointed I failed to win the jackpot because the thing is...well, that much money would probably have ruined my life.

I mean, seriously, how would I ever trust God again? I'd just trust in my bank account's ability to provide for myself and my family. I'd never know whether people listened to me because they wanted to have a constructive conversation or because they wanted something from me. I'd worry about my kids being kidnapped for ransom or seeing them affected by "affluenza."

Notch (aka Markus Alexej Persson) is the video game designer who created the game *Minecraft*. Shortly after selling his game to Microsoft for $2.5 billion, he sent out a series of tweets. Here are several quotes from his tweetstorm:

"The problem with getting everything is you run out of reasons to keep trying, and human interaction becomes impossible due to imbalance."

"Hanging out in Ibiza with a bunch of friends and partying with famous people, able to do whatever I want, and I've never felt more isolated."[3]

There's something to be learned here.

Here's a man who worked hard to create something of value in our world. Big value. And now it's hard for him to stay motivated because he has everything he wants or needs—at least everything that has a price tag.

Most of us will never have to worry about winning billions or selling something for that amount. But we all have to answer this question: How much is enough?

If a billion is more than we need, could we say the same about half of that? about a million? about one hundred thousand?

Writing in *How to Be Rich*, Andy Stanley suggests that "rich" is a moving target for humans.[4] Somehow it's always more than we have.

---

1 I agree that there are some legitimate concerns about the lottery harming people of lower income. But on the flip side, if I won, I would have been able to build a base in a dormant volcano and finally deal with that pesky James Bond.

2 I was wrong. I did win. $4.

3 Both tweets by Markus Persson (@notch), August 29, 2015.

4 Andy Stanley, *How to Be Rich* (Grand Rapids, Zondervan, 2013), 31.

Right now, I'd consider anyone with $100 million to be insanely rich. Yet if I suddenly found myself with that amount in the bank, I'd probably define "the rich" as billionaires, not millionaires like myself.

Remember Jesus' encounter with the rich young man? It's described in several of the Gospels and also makes an appearance in chapter 4 of this book.

You'll recall Jesus tells the man to sell all he has and give the proceeds to the poor, thereby launching a few thousand years of nervous wondering if we, too, need to do the same thing to please a Messiah who chose to live as a homeless man.[5]

Again, no. Jesus said that once, to one man. It wasn't a blanket statement for all Jesus-followers for all time.

Jesus *could* have delivered a hard and fast rule about how much money his followers could safely manage. Instead, he warns us against loving money no matter how much money we have: "No one can serve two masters. For you will hate one and love the other; you will be devoted to one and despise the other. You cannot serve God and be enslaved to money" (Matthew 6:24).

You see, money's not really the problem. Money becoming a distraction or obstacle between us and God—*that's* the problem. And I'll be the first to admit I've had that problem.

Over the years several external issues have negatively impacted my emotional—and spiritual—health. Money's just one of them.

At one time, it was NFL games. If my team didn't win on Sunday, Monday morning was tough. I was in a bad mood all day.

For a while I let politics and the outcome of elections dictate my mood.

And then there's the Big One: money.

I tracked my retirement account like a hawk and knew to the penny how much I made or lost on any given day. The more I had, the more pleased I felt, the more secure and accomplished.

So you can imagine my emotional and spiritual health during the economic meltdown in the 2000s.

Here's the reality: Back then I was hoarding money, caring only about how it could benefit me. I was the person Jesus was warning about loving money, about placing my trust in money rather than in him.

It didn't feel like it at the time, but I was the rich young man.

I've learned to have a healthier attitude about both money and politics (and mostly enjoy sports without getting emotionally tied up in them) and my life's better for it. I see the wisdom in Jesus' unreasonable demand to keep money in its place as a useful tool rather than a really bad master.

Here are six specific strategies that I've found combat my tendency to give money too prominent a place in my heart. See if they'll help you as well.

---

5   Matthew 8:20

Be intentionally generous.

No matter how much you have, be generous with it.

In Luke 21, Jesus commends the generosity of a woman who's desperately poor and yet gives generously of what she has.

If giving $10 a month to a worthwhile charity is difficult for you, do it and don't feel bad it isn't $100 or $1,000. And if you decide to give up Starbucks or an app download so you can make that $10 gift happen, you're working to keep money in its proper place in your heart.

As part of my detox from hoarding money, I picked charities that lined up with Jesus' words as he's quoted in Matthew 25:35-36.

Here's a quick summary: Jesus told his followers "I was hungry and you fed me…thirsty and you gave me a drink…I was naked, sick, in prison"; you remember what he said. And if you don't, feel free to reread it. It's cool. I can wait.

I chose one charity that fed people in need, one that provided clean drinking water in rural villages, and one that helped women who had been trafficked, and I started donating clothing I wasn't using to charity.

I also added charities for widows and orphans based on James 1:27: "Pure and genuine religion is the sight of God the Father means caring for orphans and widows in their distress and refusing to let the world corrupt you."

I set up recurring giving so that I'd help people on purpose, not just when I felt like it or my paycheck happened to show up fattened by some overtime hours.

Be faithful.

In the parable of the three servants,[6] Jesus describes a businessman who gives three servants money to manage. The servant with the most ability to handle finances gets five talents, the second most capable servant gets two, and the least-experienced servant receives one.

But while the amounts vary, the expectation is identical for all three servants: Be faithful in managing the money.

When the master returns, that's the standard by which he measures success. Have they been faithful? Have they used his money in the way the master would have used it had he been present?

It was okay that the servant who was given less earned less. His actions had been faithful.

That's what Jesus asks of us. His definition of success, when it comes to how you handle your money, is whether you've been faithful. Whether you use what you're given in a way that honors God and reflects his values.

Stay aware.

About 29,000 children die in our world each day from preventable causes like

---

6   Matthew 25:14-30

starvation and diarrhea.[7] Those of us who can afford to purchase books or subscribe to Netflix are well off by any measure, even if others around us have more.

And one way to keep a healthy view of money is to stay aware of needs in other parts of our world.

I'm not saying to feel bad about your car, your phone, or any other use of your income. Shame isn't a tool that will ever bring restoration to our broken world.

I'm simply saying that we often feel sorry for ourselves, and that's seldom appropriate. When you broaden your perspective, you'll discover you may, in fact, live in extraordinary abundance. That realization makes it easier to share with others.

So read the uncomfortable profiles about poverty in Haiti. Add a few informative documentaries to your queue even if they make you squirm. Look at pictures of refugee camps from time to time.[8]

Stay aware—and let that awareness shape you.

Faith > Money

Consider this passage written by the Apostle Peter to Christians who were worried about lots of problems—some of those problems financial: "These trials will show that your faith is genuine. It is being tested as fire tests and purifies gold—though your faith is far more precious than mere gold" (1 Peter 1:7).

Notice the implication of what Peter's saying: If God has to choose, he'd rather you have faith than money. In the Kingdom's economy, faith is far more valuable than money.

So it's not a stretch to think that, perhaps, God uses financial stress to help increase our faith.

If you're like me, you never pray more than when you're in a position of need. We tend to turn to God most fervently when we're marching toward some sort of cliff—financial or otherwise.

More times than I care to recount, money's been a center-stage concern in my life. Each time God has provided, but I still feel anxious when my savings seem insufficient to handle unexpected expenses that may or may not occur.

I want to use money to control my world, but God's priority is that I trust him.

So how do I make the shift from trusting money to trusting God instead?

In Philippians 4, Paul shares his answer to that question. He says he can deal with plenty or poverty, but not because of his willpower. Rather, it's because of strength God provides.

---

7   http://www.unicef.org/mdg/childmortality.html
8   The cute kitty pictures will still be there when you're done, I promise.

Paul can avoid wallowing in worry because he has confidence in God. He doesn't look at his situation but keeps his eyes on God—and relies on God's strength.

Choose trust rather than control.

Trusting in God doesn't necessarily mean loving the painful situations in which we sometimes find ourselves. Jesus clearly didn't love the hours of agony and abandonment he faced while he prayed in the garden of Gethsemane.

Paul wasn't hoping for more shipwrecks and stonings.

I don't want my car to break down, either, or for my daughter to have a hard time at school. But the question is whether those things loom larger in my mind than God's goodness and his sovereignty. That is, the reality that he's in control and cares about me.

Because if issues and problems loom larger in my eyes than God's ability to control them, then they'll have a greater influence in my life than God has. And this is what noted and respected biblical scholars refer to as a "spectacularly bad idea."

I've already admitted it: I like being in control. Raise your hand if that's you, too.[9]

There's nothing wrong with making plans and preparations, but if our plans ignore the nature of God (all-powerful, all-knowing, all-present), how much good will our plans really do for us?

When it comes to finances, I think Paul lobs us a softball in Philippians 4:6-7: "Don't worry about anything; instead, pray about everything. Tell God what you need, and thank him for all he has done. Then you will experience God's peace, which exceeds anything we can understand. His peace will guard your hearts and minds as you live in Christ Jesus."

I like to boil this down to a pseudo-mathematical formula:

Prayer + Thanks = Peace.

By "prayer," I think Paul's simply reinforcing a truth Jesus shares in his sermon: We can trust God to provide what we need. Instead of carrying the weight of an unending stream of "what ifs," we can entrust them to a loving God.

Your Father hasn't forgotten or abandoned you when your finances are rocky. He promises to give you strength.

And when it comes to thanks, if you're following Jesus, I'm guessing you have a story or two about instances where things seemed bleak but, in the end, they worked out.

Maybe that's part of your salvation experience.

Maybe you've seen that play out in your finances.

---

9   Now throw your other hand in the air. Now wave them like you just don't care. Now hop on one foot. Now do the cupid shuffle. I promise, I'm in counseling for my control issues.

When you're struggling to trust God, do this: Intentionally recall those stories. Listen to yourself tell them to others.

Remember, in addition to loving you, God's invested a great deal into you—he's not about to kick you to the curb.

Paul says to thank God for what he has done. I think we can safely add to that advice that we can give thanks—in advance—for what he'll do.

The outcome: a peace that is completely unreasonable.

In fact, Jesus says his peace goes beyond all understanding, so it's clear our ability to stop worrying isn't linked to our ability to figure stuff out. For me, my anxiety (financial and otherwise) is directly linked to my ability to comprehend the "master plan." If I'm honest here, I have to admit I find myself saying stuff like "I'm trusting God; I just want to know what he's up to."

I don't think that sort of conditional trust is what Jesus is suggesting will banish worry. Our ability to stop worrying is linked to trusting God. Period.

So times of uncertainty—including those that involve the stock market—are chances for our faith to deepen.

Remember who's in control.

Dr. Henry Cloud, writing in the *Boundaries* book series, suggests we don't control other people.[10] We may also have little or no control over situations we face, but we *can* control ourselves.

Dr. Emmerson Eggerichs, writing in *Love and Respect*, says it this way: "My response is my responsibility."[11]

And Jesus—you remember Jesus[12]—says this: There will be trouble in this world.[13] As in, you can expect challenges. Loving and following him doesn't remove you from experiencing life's rocky patches.

Add that up and you get this: When hard days arrive, and they will, you can choose to respond in the healthiest way possible. The most faithful way possible. And, in Jesus' view, worrying isn't a part of the equation.

The equation is this: Prayer + Thanks = Peace.

So pick your master: God or money. Decide who you'll trust more: God or yourself. Make your plans, map out your strategies, and stop worrying about what you'll do if bad things happen.

Because *bad things will happen.*

Jesus confirms as much.

Money doesn't give a rip about you. Much better, in my view, to trust in the God who loves you enough to give you peace and point you toward a fulfilling life whether you're dirt poor or professional-athlete rich.

---

10   Henry Cloud and John Townsend, *Boundaries* (Grand Rapids, Zondervan, 1992).

11   Emerson Eggerichs, *Love and Respect* (Nashville, W. Publishing Group, 2004), 284.

12   About yay tall, brown skin, good with carpentry tools...

13   John 16:33

▌▌ A Brief Pause

Don't worry about money…That's a good one, Jesus. Wait…you're *serious*?

Just for fun, if I gave you a million dollars, what would you do with it?

_____

_____

_____

_____

How does Jesus' expectation that we trust him more than money strike you? What can you point to in your life that demonstrates your ability to do it…or not?

_____

_____

_____

_____

What does Jesus reveal about himself in this portion of his sermon?

_____

_____

_____

_____

Chapter 12

DON'T JUDGE OTHERS

*Do not judge others, and you will not be
judged. For you will be treated as you treat
others. The standard you use in judging is
the standard by which you will be judged.*

*And why worry about a speck in your friend's eye
when you have a log in your own? How can you
think of saying to your friend, "Let me help you get
rid of that speck in your eye," when you can't see
past the log in your own eye? Hypocrite! First get
rid of the log in your own eye; then you will see well
enough to deal with the speck in your friend's eye.*

*Don't waste what is holy on people who are
unholy. Don't throw your pearls to pigs! They will
trample the pearls, then turn and attack you.*

—Matthew 7:1-6

In her book *Take This Bread*, Sara Miles describes her journey of becoming
a believer in Jesus at the age of 46. As a "secular intellectual journalist with
a habit of skepticism," she'd seen many terrible things, especially during the
wars and strife in Nicaragua, El Salvador, the Philippines, and South Africa.

She looked to activism to bring solutions to the terrible challenges
in human society: homelessness, abuse, war, and hunger, among others.

When she took a close look at Christianity, instead of the flawed political organization some sectors of the church have become, Miles saw something different:

"I stumbled into a radically inclusive faith centered on sacraments and action...I discovered a religion rooted in the most ordinary yet subversive practice: a dinner table where everyone is welcome, where the despised and outcasts are honored."[1]

I love Miles' description of the core of Christianity: a place anyone can find community. A place judgment is suspended but grace isn't. And there can be no doubt that those values can be traced straight back to the example of Jesus himself.

Consider Jesus' first interaction with a man who'll become one of his 12 apostles: Matthew.

Matthew is a tax collector. That means he's basically a traitor and a thief because he's collecting taxes for an occupying Roman government. Excited that Jesus wants anything to do with him at all, Matthew throws a party and invites Jesus, the other disciples, plus pretty much everybody Matthew knows.

The issue is that the only people Matthew knows are outcasts like himself— other tax collectors, probably some prostitutes, maybe a few thugs who help out with "collections."

That's the group of people Jesus is hanging out with when the Pharisees ask the rest of the disciples, "Why does your teacher eat with such scum?" (Matthew 9:11).

Most of us probably have at least one story we could tell about a time religious people made us feel like scum.

I certainly have.

When I was attending a Bible college in Dallas, I was asked to lead music at a small local church while their regular guy was out of town.

After a couple of weeks, the pastor tells me their music leader is moving soon and asks me to take over on a weekly basis. I agree to do so.

Later that week, I schedule a meeting with that pastor. I tell him I'm having trouble with a particular sin.

I've been looking at some stuff on the internet I shouldn't be viewing. As a married seminary student, my guilt is painful and overwhelming. I've tried to keep this secret from everyone, but finally I've hit a point where I'm desperate for help.

So I confess my sin to the pastor.

After I leave his office, he never speaks to me again. The next week, I'm informed that I'm no longer welcome to lead music, and the pastor's wife tells my wife that she should leave me.

---

1   Sara Miles, *Take This Bread* (New York, Ballantine Books, 2007), xii-xiii.

Thankfully, my wife didn't listen, and eventually I learned to walk in the freedom that Jesus offers me and everyone else. That sin's now in the rearview mirror.

After that experience, I was pretty well done with church. I didn't regularly attend any church for years. By his actions, that pastor labeled me as scum, unworthy of love or care. I certainly didn't enjoy the feeling of being judged by someone in a place of spiritual authority.[2]

But, years later, I became part of the problem before I decided to become part of the solution.

Following Bible college, I attended graduate school to study Scripture and theology at a deeper level. I gradually got to the point where I wasn't sure if others really "understood" the Christian life the way I understood it, and I was quick to criticize people who were "doing it wrong."

I wouldn't have admitted it to anybody at the time (especially myself), but I was miserable, and I'm pretty sure I made lots of other people miserable as well. I'd become like the pastor who'd tried to shame me. I'd become like the religious people who couldn't understand why Jesus would want to be around "scum."

I'll never forget the day when, during prayer, I felt as if God took a wrecking ball to the prison of self-righteousness and hypocrisy I'd built around myself. I'd carefully constructed it, brick by brick, but he leveled it all.

God showed me a freedom I'd lost in the midst of all my rule-keeping and striving, and I vowed never to go back to living like the Pharisees who attacked Jesus.

In the Bible we see Jesus accept imperfect people. He accepts them without endorsing their behavior, and that's where I want to be as well.

The Pharisees refuse to deal with broken, flawed people—even though that's *exactly* what they are themselves. Somehow, the irony is lost on them.

Here are a handful of truths I've found helpful in reining in my inner Pharisee, in helping me judge others by a yardstick I won't mind having applied to myself.

The Gospel is good news, not a rule book.

Jesus is always far more accepting than people around him find comfortable. On more than one occasion, even his own disciples were confused about why Jesus was interacting with questionable outsiders.[3] Which was funny, given that they themselves were absolutely *not* the kind of people a renowned rabbi would normally select as followers.

---

2 Many years later, I reached out to that pastor to offer him forgiveness. He didn't remember me and didn't offer any sort of apology. Fortunately, my choice to forgive him wasn't dependent on his actions or attitude. And my view of God is no longer influenced by the flaws in other people. I'm too busy being grateful that God loves me in the midst of my shortcomings.

3 John 4:27; Matthew 15:21-28

The Kingdom of God is a party everyone is invited to. Christians aren't the designated bouncers at the door; we're the promoters busy getting the word out to everyone.[4]

In Galatians 2:18, Paul writes, "I am a sinner if I rebuild the old system of law I already tore down." If we just create new "Jesus rules" or standards someone has to meet before we let them into our Christian camp, we're completely missing the point of why Jesus was born, lived, died, and lived again.

No one ever has to be an outsider again. That's the wonderful news Jesus announces in his sermon and then makes possible through his sacrifice on the cross.

I previously mentioned that I've run a number of adventure races in the past several years. Those are races in which you have to overcome obstacles during a run that typically lasts anywhere from 3 to 15 miles.

In one particularly popular adventure race, they always save a specific obstacle for near the end of the course: a large quarter pipe called Everest. Imagine that you've been running for several hours and you're beyond exhausted. Then, at about the 13-mile marker, you have to find the energy to run up a ramp that turns into a 15-foot-high vertical wall.

And because everyone ahead of you has had to scale the same obstacle, it's wet and muddy.

Almost no runners can clear the obstacle on their own, which leads to one of my favorite parts of the event: Strangers lie on the top of the obstacle and reach down to help the next man or woman coming up the slope. Muddy, sometimes bloody, hands reach up and discover another hand waiting for them to grab.

One runner scrambles to scale the wall, doing his best to find any foothold while above him another runner strains with all her might to pull him up to the top.

There are no outsiders in this moment, just a mass of humanity working together to overcome a great challenge.

The loudest cheers at that obstacle are for people who have tried unsuccessfully to make it up several times but finally grab hold of one of the hands and claw their way up over the edge.

In some ways, that moment is as perfect an image of the church as any Sunday service I've ever been part of.

I love to imagine Jesus as being the only guy who could make it up to the ledge on his own and then, instead of taking off, he reaches down, willing to get filthy as he helps others make it to the level only he was able to reach.

There's no critique of climbing technique—just help.

No tut-tutting about where you are in the race—just help.

No judgment—just help.

---

4   Matthew 28:18-20

And because of what he's done for me, I, too, lie down on the ledge and reach down to grab hold of whoever needs me.

Acceptance isn't the same thing as approval.

More than once, Jesus ends an encounter with some version of "go and sin no more."[5] The difference between how Jesus says this and what we in the church tend to do is that Jesus admonished others in the context of relationship, not rules.

It was only after Jesus demonstrated how much he valued people that he held them accountable for the sin that held them captive.

It's the same for us.

We can only hold people accountable to the extent that we have influence with them. Influence comes from relationship, and relationship is gained by demonstrating genuine care over the course of time.

To say it another way, if I'm walking about the mall and a complete stranger comes up to me and says, "That haircut absolutely does not work for you," I'll probably give him a funny look and keep walking. If, on the other hand, my wife tells me the same thing, I'm probably going to pay attention.[6] I know my wife is telling me out of a place of genuine care.

My buddy Chris once convinced a friend to go to church with him. Chris' friend hadn't been in church since childhood. No sooner had Chris and his friend found seats than someone sitting behind them leaned forward and chastised Chris' friend for wearing a hat in church. Embarrassed, the young man removed his hat…and never returned.

Jesus' unreasonable demand that we're as accepting of others as we want Jesus to be of us would have been helpful here in a big way.

When Jesus told people to leave their sinful lives, I don't think it came across as a threat or a criticism, but rather as a caution: "Hey, I want you to have a better life. Stop doing things that just end up hurting you."

If we want to be effective at discipleship—a fancy word for "helping people follow Jesus"—we need to first and foremost love well, and let that love inform the teaching, coaching, and correcting that comes with making disciples.[7]

We don't know the full story, but God does.

Jesus says there will be surprises when the Kingdom of God fully arrives— surprises regarding who'll be the most honored.[8] I believe there may be a number of ushers in local churches who'll be honored above the men and women who spend the most time on stage.

---

5   John 5:14; John 8:11

6   I MEAN DEFINITELY. DEFINITELY PAY ATTENTION!

7   By the way, one of the last things Matthew records Jesus saying before he ascends into heaven is that we should make disciples (Matthew 28:19). So we probably want to take this unreasonable challenge seriously…

8   Matthew 7:21-23; Matthew 19:30

In this portion of his sermon, Jesus warns his audience to not be hypocritical judges. The truth is that our ability to gauge who does and doesn't have it all together is probably not terribly well calibrated. People we point to as distinctly imperfect may be closer to the Kingdom than we ourselves are.

We expect God to show us tremendous grace because he loves us, and I, for one, am all in favor of that. But we sometimes forget what Peter once said: "God shows no favoritism" (Acts 10:34). That same insane, undeserved—dare I say unreasonable—grace that God shows me, he shows to *all* his sons and daughters.

When I keep that in mind, it's easier to love others…and judge them less harshly.

Shouldn't we Christians be more accepting of outcasts than anybody else? After all, we were all outcasts ourselves. *We* were the scum. *We* were the people slamming up against the wall, hopeless in reaching the top until Jesus grabbed our outstretched hands and pulled us up and over.

I'm thinking that experience might lead us to feel compassion, not disdain, for those who *are now* where we *were*.

We'll never judge anyone into the Kingdom. What draws others in is what drew us to Jesus: love.

And if Jesus is serious about what he's saying in his sermon, he's not interested in our judgment creating a barrier between him and the people he's leaning down to pull up and over the ledge with the rest of us.

Let's be the ones cheering the loudest, both with encouragement for the weary people climbing the wall and with celebration for everyone who lets Jesus offer a helping hand.

▌▌ A Brief Pause

Judging others may be a reflex action for you—it was for me. Yet Jesus expects us to withhold judgment or to at least recognize that whatever yardstick we apply to others will be applied to us.

What can we learn about Jesus as we consider this portion of his sermon? What's he telling us about himself?

_____

_____

_____

What's he telling us about us?

_____

_____

_____

_____

If church people have ever made you feel like scum, how did you deal with it?

_____

_____

_____

_____

Chapter 13
EFFECTIVE PRAYER

Keep on asking, and you will receive what you ask for. Keep on seeking, and you will find. Keep on knocking, and the door will be opened to you. For everyone who asks, receives. Everyone who seeks, finds. And to everyone who knocks, the door will be opened.

You parents—if your children ask for a loaf of bread, do you give them a stone instead? Or if they ask for a fish, do you give them a snake? Of course not! So if you sinful people know how to give good gifts to your children, how much more will your heavenly Father give good gifts to those who ask him.

—Matthew 7:7-11

Can we be honest for a moment?

Sometimes life is just gonna stink. You'll be happily skipping along, and then something will blindside you and knock you flat.

- A relationship breakup torpedoes you.

- A health issue pops up and threatens you or a loved one.

- You lose your job.

- You're struggling with an addiction or other major issue that you just can't get on top of.

And if you're a parent, you have days when your kids have decided to drive you insane. Those are not easy days.

Recently, my three children were having a full-fledged drive-Mom-and-Dad-nuts day. So I took them on a walk deep into the local woods where I made them pledge to be respectful and obedient *forever* before I'd agree to lead them back home. My kids know me well enough that they were smiling as I took a picture of their raised right hands during their vow so I could share it on social media.[1]

I sincerely wish that when we decide to follow Jesus, we could be sure things would automatically go smoother for us. That because I'm a Jesus-follower my kids would always listen. That my car would never need a mechanic. That my co-workers would always be nice to me.

I try to be kind to others, I read my Bible regularly, I give to my church and to charities, yet I often feel as if life is a boxing match where I'm in the 12th round against a heavyweight.

And in the midst of this struggle, Jesus tells me to trust God. To continue to hope in God's promises. To keep knocking at God's door. To keep seeking.

When I'm slogging through one hardship after another, this seems more than just a little unreasonable.

Doesn't God…I don't know…kind of…*owe* me? At least a *little*?

I mean, listen, I know Jesus went to the cross for me and I can never pay him back for that. I get that, and I'm so grateful. But shouldn't I get to avoid some of the issues other people deal with because I'm on board with what God asks me to do?

Apparently not.

And I'm reminded of my least favorite promise in the Gospels, one I've mentioned before. In John 16:33, Jesus says this: "Here on earth you will have many trials and sorrows…"

Jesus doesn't say, "you *might* have trouble" or "*if* you have trouble." Instead, he guarantees it: We *will* have trouble. But shouldn't that trouble at least be little stuff like maybe somebody telling me I'm dumb for believing in Jesus? Something manageable, something that doesn't really *hurt*?

I've served in various ministry roles for years, and I've talked with tons of people dealing with illness, financial problems, addictions, and everything else you can name. We've lost several church members to cancer in my time. I've had to do a funeral for a two-day-old baby.

And those are just the difficulties I hear about.

I also have challenges in my own life that just make life hard. My wife and I are still dealing with the financial fallout from the failure of a business we believe God told us to buy years ago. Having a child with special needs is a never-ending battle in numerous ways.

---

1   For a modest fee, and ironclad legal waiver, I will happily march your children into the woods and do the same thing. You just say the word.

My wife and I occasionally talk about whether we'll ever get to a point where life isn't just so dang hard.

Shouldn't we get off better than the rest of society because we're working to be obedient to Jesus? Shouldn't this healthier, fuller life Jesus talks about in John 10:10 be a little cushier?

It doesn't feel reasonable to me that I should put others first; earnestly try to honor God; sacrifice time, money, and energy to God's Kingdom…and then still deal with the same junk everybody else faces.

This portion of Jesus' sermon is usually quoted when people preach about God's generosity and having persistence in prayer. And those concepts are certainly present.

But one thing I love about the words of Jesus is that there are often multiple ways we can apply the truths he shares.

Yes, God is generous. Yes, be persistent in prayer. Yes, give good gifts to your children, like God gives good gifts to us.

But did you notice? There's a whole lot of asking going on. A whole lot of someone wanting something.

And, at least in my life (you're above this, I know), much of my asking, knocking, and seeking is motivated by a rather well-rounded sense of self-centeredness.

I'm not asking, knocking, and seeking on behalf of others. Or for the betterment of the world.

It's all about me. Or, in your case, you.

Jesus' words here in this portion of his sermon prompted me to explore my self-centeredness (it can get ugly) and led to two flashes of understanding.

See if these might also speak to you…

First, God's all about building your faith.

Listen, if everybody who decided to follow Jesus got a Tesla, lost 30 pounds, and landed their dream job, who *wouldn't* follow Jesus? And how would it be possible to take seriously Jesus' admonition to pick up our cross and follow him?

Forget unreasonable. It would be impossible.

I don't know about you, but it's when everything is going well that I actually have the *hardest* time drawing closer to Jesus.

I suspect he occasionally allows my life to catch some chaos to help me remain engaged in discipleship—the process of growing closer to him.

The fuller, healthier life Jesus refers to in his sermon involves so much more than money and possessions. It's about a life of more meaning. Those "good gifts" God gives may not always show up on a bank statement.

Am I willing to trust God to bless me, even when it's not in the manner I'd prefer? even if his "good gifts" don't look like what I'm expecting?

Or am I only in this thing for what I can get out of it? The Scriptures repeatedly affirm that we are called to patiently have faith when dealing with doubt or when we don't feel fulfilled.[2]

Will we trust God to fulfill his promises to us when all the evidence we see points to the contrary? The name for that is "faith," perhaps even "unreasonable faith."

Heck, sometimes I'm pretty sure "faith" and "unreasonable" are synonyms.

Second, there's an enemy at work.

In Matthew 13:24-30, there's a story about a farmer planting his fields with good seed. During the night, an enemy sows weeds among the crops. By the time the farm workers figure it out, there's nothing they can do. Pulling up the weeds will damage the crops, so the farmer decides to let the weeds grow. He'll separate the weeds from the crop come harvest time.

Writing in *Strength to Love*, Martin Luther King Jr. explains his take on this story. King notes that Jesus never disputes the reality of evil. He doesn't say the weeds were an illusion or a state of mind. He says the weeds are real, as evil is real.[3]

King, like Jesus, acknowledges that there's hard stuff in life, evil stuff.

And King points to the other message in Jesus' story: God is going to deal with evil once and for all at the time of the harvest. That's when he'll deal with the enemy—Satan—along with all the work Satan's kingdom has been up to.

But in the meantime, this side of the harvest, Satan is someone Jesus calls the "ruler of this world."[4]

Yes, the Kingdom of God is here—but it hasn't yet fully arrived. We can't expect a world that is clearly not paradise to treat us as though it were.

That's not an unreasonable expectation; it's an impossible one.

When I keep these two truths in mind—that God's looking for faith and there's an enemy at work, it prepares me to deal with life. It helps me see that when Jesus points me toward the unreasonable, maybe in some cases it's because the alternative is impossible.

God has promised abundant life, and he'll deliver it. That's a promise I believe, so I'll put everything I have into getting myself in position to receive it.

That's one reason Jesus includes these words about prayer in his sermon. When life is hard, when you aren't getting what you need, when nobody seems to care about you, and you're not sure what to do next, Jesus says, "Keep going. Keep seeking. Keep asking. Keep knocking. You have a Father who'll never give up on you or ignore you, no matter what your circumstances seem to say."

---

2   James 1:12; Revelation 2:10; Matthew 25:1-13
3   King, *Strength to Love*.
4   John 12:31

Furthermore, there's really no benefit in wasting bandwidth freaking out. One consequence of the Holy Spirit being active in our lives is our experiencing peace. Another is that we grow in patience.[5]

Paul writes that he's figured out how to be content in any situation and then backs up his words by singing praises while chained up in a dungeon.[6]

Joseph stays faithful to God while spending years in prison for a crime he didn't commit.

Job...I mean what can you say? This guy, in the midst of a specific and directed attack by the devil, refuses to curse God. *Despite* the fact that he knows he doesn't deserve his treatment.

So does that mean Jesus expects us to keep a stiff upper lip, have unquestioning blind faith, and, above all, *never* say or write things like "Sometimes life is just gonna stink"? Even if we've spent days, weeks, or perhaps years in some holding pattern or barren wasteland?

Here's what I've learned about seeking, asking, and knocking during my times in the wasteland: You grow *way* more in the wasteland than anywhere else. There's a benefit to those times in your life when it seems like all the marrow has been sucked from your bones. When life seems to be only shades of gray rather than vibrant color. When the soundtrack of life is more like fingernails on a chalkboard than a tuned-up orchestra.

When life is good and well and easy, it's easy to coast.

But not when you're in the wasteland.

I've completed a few off-road triathlons.[7] During the bike-ride portion, some stretches are flat and easy. It's hard for me to push myself to the breaking point in those sections of a triathlon. Usually, I'm content to hold back and just pedal at a normal pace.

But in those sections that are steep, covered in loose rocks and dirt, filled with deep pits and large, sharp rocks that want nothing more than to wreck my bike, I don't need any extra motivation to go all out. There's no temptation to coast because I can't. The only way I can climb those insanely tough stretches is by giving more than I thought I had to give.

Those are the worst parts of the race, and they're exactly the same parts that make completing the race worthwhile. Later, when I talk about the race, I don't tell people about the easy stuff. I talk about the parts that nearly broke me but that I somehow overcame.

It's overcoming the hardest challenges the course can throw at me that makes the accomplishment of completing the course worthwhile.

---

5   Galatians 5:22-23
6   Acts 16:25
7   You may be getting tired of me talking about various races and events. Rest assured my wife is, too, so you're in good company. But let's be honest: Half the reason to do cool events is so you can say you've done cool events. Fine, 95 percent of the reason.

It's the same in life. When, by God's grace and mercy, you make it through the darkest days, the uncertain days, the days where hope seems to be a cruel weapon rather than the rope that keeps you from falling, *those* are the days that define who you are. Those are the days that strip away the things holding you back, keeping you complacent.

I didn't want to spend two years of my life being refined and prepared for full-time ministry. I see in retrospect that God did exactly what needed to be done. Only he knows what changes need to occur in my life, so only he is qualified to place me in situations where those changes can happen.

Like me, you might want to be used by God to help heal this broken world. But part of the deal of being *used* by God is being *prepared* by God.

Even Jesus spent 40 days without food in the desert after waiting 30 years to start his public ministry. And how much more do I need to be prepared than Jesus?

So when life's hard, remember how God has been faithful to you, even (especially?) when you didn't deserve it. These seasons are a chance to reflect some of that faithfulness back to God. To honor the God who never leaves you or forsakes you.

So in those times I don't understand why God is allowing something in my life—I don't get into my first-choice school, or I don't land that job I think will be a perfect fit—it's an opportunity to worship God by being faithful.

And above all, to never give up.

▊▊ A Brief Pause

Knock…seek…be persistent…and the door will be opened. But it may *not* be the door to an easy life. That's the news Jesus shares, and no matter how we feel about it, it's good news.

Jesus is telling us something about himself and the Kingdom of God in this part of his sermon. What do you hear in his words?

_____

_____

_____

Thinking about your life, has your faith grown more during the good times or during the not-so-good times?

_____

_____

_____

_____

What do you think about this statement: "Difficult times are an opportunity to reflect the faithfulness God has shown to me back to him"?

_____

_____

_____

_____

Chapter 14

THE GOLDEN RULE

Do to others whatever you would like them
to do to you. This is the essence of all that
is taught in the law and the prophets.

—*Matthew 7:12*

Let me tell you about a next-door neighbor I once had. His name was Glen.

Glen's favorite pastime was screaming f-bombs at his wife while my kids were playing outside.

That's probably not true, but some days it definitely felt like it.

One of the highlights of living next to Glen included having the cops show up to ask my wife if she'd seen Glen because he'd been driving around the neighborhood boosting Christmas decorations off other people's lawns.

Another was the time our next-door neighbors (on the other side) decided to sell their house. It was a tough market, so they didn't get much attention. But one sunny day a prospective buyer showed up to take a look around.

Glen decided that was the right time to go change the oil in his truck. Wearing only pajama bottoms. While shouting obscenities at his wife who was 50 feet away in their house at the time. Oddly enough, the prospective buyer didn't put a contract on the house.

Those neighbors still live next to us.

Glen's kids frequently used my car as a backstop when they were playing baseball, despite my asking them not to.

Not long ago, Glen and his family moved away. I can't tell you how happy my wife and I were about this. He didn't ask, but I would have cheerfully helped load the moving truck.

Here's the twist in this story: I failed Glen.

I didn't treat him the way I want to be treated. See, I want people to give me loads of grace to cover over those parts of my life that are a mess. Yet I had no interest in extending that same line of credit to Glen and his family.

Jesus sets an unreasonable expectation that I'll love my neighbor as myself. He says it's a summary statement of the law and prophets. But even though I want my neighbors to love me, I didn't choose to love Glen.

I know that stepping up and accepting Jesus' challenge to love my neighbors, fueled by the transforming power of the Holy Spirit, will make this a better world. If I'm nice only to people who are easy to be nice to, this world is never going to change.

Jesus tells a story about the "good Samaritan" that I won't repeat in detail because it's one of the most recognized stories Jesus ever shared. Though if you happen to not know it, you can find it in Luke 10:25-37.

In short, the main points: Jewish guy gets mugged and beaten. Several Jewish religious leaders pass by, unwilling to help. Along comes Samaritan outsider who helps lavishly, leading to a question: Who was the real neighbor in this situation? And the answer (spoiler alert): The Samaritan because he's the one who helped.

I look at that story and see this: Jesus wants us to create community any time we get the opportunity, even if that opportunity is with our enemies.[1]

I never looked for chances to create community with Glen and his family. I never invited his family over to toast marshmallows when we were 20 feet from his front door. Never offered to play catch with the kids that were growing up in what I knew to be a stressful household.

I chose instead to express my frustration with glares and head shakes.

Our world didn't get any better because of how I acted.

And this isn't only about Glen. Every time I ignore the opportunity to create community, I'm just letting things stay the way they are.

I wanted my neighborhood to be more connected, but I wasn't willing to do anything about it.

I'm an introvert, and it's easy for me to treat the cashier at the grocery store as if he or she is a piece of furniture. Social interaction takes effort, and I just want to go home. But in that moment, loving my neighbor means looking the cashier in the eye, taking a moment to say "thanks," and generally treating the cashier like a human.

Instead of slamming a troll on Twitter or Facebook, it means saying something like "Tell me more about why you think that."

And rather than excuse my nasty comments and rude actions toward someone I don't like, Jesus seems to expect me to actually care for that person.

That story about the Samaritan, if I take it seriously, strips away all my arguments in which I justify my refusal to reach out to those who are

---

1   Because of this story, we think good things when we hear the word *Samaritan*. But in Jesus' day, his Jewish crowd despised them. Imagine me going to the Republican National Convention and telling a story where Republicans were the bad guys and the good guy was a Democrat (or vice versa). The story would not be received well. That's the kind of status-quo challenging Jesus is doing here.

different from me. Jesus' sermon, if I take it seriously, gives me zero room to rationalize away my rudeness toward people I just don't like.

Jesus expects me to be kind and considerate to those who don't look like me, believe what I believe, or think like I think.

If you're like me, and you want this world to be a better place than it currently is, I hope you'll take Jesus at his word.

I'm actually grateful for Glen. Glen showed me that I had a problem, and I decided not to ignore it. I'm now working on getting to know my neighbors, even the ones I didn't particularly want to get to know, and now we've started to build connections with one another.

I'm now building a community with my neighbors, and I think the world is just a little better for it. My neighborhood certainly is.

Here are some practical steps I recommend if you're interested in living out the whole "treat others the way you want to be treated" idea with your neighbors.

Go meet them.

Maybe it would be awkward to randomly knock on a neighbor's door and announce to whoever opens it that you want to meet whoever answers your knock. Especially if they've lived near you for…oh, let's call it a year or more.

Fortunately, there are a few times each year when knocking on those doors is socially acceptable.

I launched my efforts by taking a small present to each of my neighbors at Christmas. I introduced myself and my family and learned the names of the families I'd failed to connect with for—in some cases—multiple years.

To make sure I didn't forget names, I wrote them down—after walking away from their doorsteps, of course. (It would have been weird to write their names down in the moment like I was a well-organized stalker. Don't be weird.)

Set up an event.

After meeting neighbors at Christmas, I hosted an Easter egg hunt on my lawn that following Easter. We invited every family with kids living near us to be part of the event. Everyone showed up. It was great. And now the neighbors weren't just meeting me; they also met each other.

After that, one of our neighbors offered his pool for a pool party later in the summer.

The second year we did the egg hunt, people stayed around and talked for hours after the event. Hours.

It's a lot easier to love people when you know their names and a bit about their lives. It's easier to treat them in ways you'd like to be treated yourself.

Decide to think the best of other people.

Maybe treating others the way you want to be treated isn't about meeting people you don't know. Maybe you have neighbors or co-workers you've met and you just don't like them. How can you hit reset on that relationship so you can replace the unhealthy with the healthy?

I suggest that it starts with deciding (and it *is* a decision) to change your mindset.

Maybe there's a history preventing you from connecting. Maybe, in your mind, the person has said or done something that needs to be made right before you'll make room in your life for the person. Or you've said or done something—and you're embarrassed about it.

Decide to wipe the ledger clean. Choose to think the best about the other person.

Nobody wakes up asking how they can make your life miserable. The lady at work who drives you nuts has her own life to worry about. Glen next door is just trying to survive from one day to the next. The person who cut you off on the highway and then flipped you off has some emotional growth to attend to.

And if you don't have any negative history with your neighbors, do everything in your power to avoid writing one.

Our new next-door neighbors (the ones who live in the house where Glen's family once lived) recently adopted a dog. At least it *looked* like a dog. It may have been a rooster because every morning at sunrise it started barking incessantly. As a heavy sleeper I didn't notice, but my wife was losing hours of sleep.

What would you do in this situation? Seethe silently? Fantasize about ways to teach them a lesson?

We were determined not to make the same mistake we'd made with Glen. Fortunately, we'd already met these neighbors a few times and knew their names. We decided to assume the best—they probably had no idea how the barking bothered us.

So one evening my wife knocked on our neighbors' door and had a friendly conversation with the young husband. I'd offered to go along, but my wife wanted to avoid making it feel like we were ganging up on whoever answered the door.[2]

Our neighbor was horrified to hear of how we were being affected, and he had no clue prior to being told. I honestly have no idea what steps they took, but the dog is still there and he doesn't bark at sunrise anymore.

My point: A situation that could have caused a relational breakdown with our neighbors was resolved because we assumed the best about them and gave them a chance to prove us right instead of filing a police complaint or being passive-aggressive about it.

We treated our neighbors the same way we'd like to be treated.

---

2   "Well, okay, if you think that's best, dear," I said, tossing my Louisville Slugger back in the closet. I'm joking. Like directions, I've learned to listen to my wife about handling social situations.

Like us, those people bear the image of God. Your neighbors bear the same image. If you're angry that they're not perfect, let that be a prompt that reminds you you're not perfect, either.

When we screw up, when we're selfish, when we behave in uncaring or inconsiderate ways, we want grace. So give it to others.

And that starts with a decision to give other people a break. To treat them the way we'd like to be treated ourselves.

It may be an unreasonable expectation from an unreasonable Savior, but there it is: Jesus is holding us to the same standard he lived out.

 A Brief Pause

Is there anything more unreasonable or idealistic than the golden rule? Yet Jesus hands it to us without any exit ramp—it's something we're to walk out, no matter what.

What does this portion of his sermon tell you about Jesus?

_____

_____

_____

Let's talk neighbors. List the names of the people who live closest to you here:

_____

_____

_____

_____

How do you feel about your ability to write…or not write…a list?
Do you have any less-than-perfect history with any neighbor that you could choose to let go and start over?

_____

_____

_____

_____

Chapter 15
THE NARROW GATE

You can enter God's Kingdom only through the narrow gate. The highway to hell is broad, and its gate is wide for the many who choose that way. But the gateway to life is very narrow and the road is difficult, and only a few ever find it.

—*Matthew 7:13-14*

I noticed something in the Bible recently: Jesus didn't take shortcuts. He was born as a baby instead of materializing as a man.

When Jesus asked John to baptize him, John thought it was crazy.[1] Jesus' response? "It should be done, for we must carry out all that God requires" (Matthew 3:15). In other words, this is the plan God laid out, so we're gonna do it right.

Later, Jesus tells the disciples that he could call down angels to rescue him from the Crucifixion at any moment...yet he doesn't do it.[2]

There are no shortcuts in faith.

You can't get to resurrection without going through crucifixion.

That's how it is with narrow paths and narrow gates: There's no easy way, no workaround. Resurrection doesn't undo the Crucifixion; it completes it.

When John writes of his heavenly vision in the book of Revelation, we see the population of heaven repeatedly referring to the sacrifice Jesus made. At one point, they sing, "Worthy is the Lamb who was slaughtered—to receive power and riches and wisdom and strength and honor and glory and blessing" (Revelation 5:12).

This isn't some kind of celebration over Jesus being a victim. Jesus wasn't a victim; he willingly sacrificed himself, and that sacrifice made him worthy of all these accolades. Because Jesus didn't bail out or take some cheap

---

1   I bet the guy asked to do his bris had to take a few deep breaths first, too.
2   Matthew 26:53

shortcut, he becomes, as one song says, "the darling of heaven."[3] He walked the path nobody else could to make it possible for us to follow him.

Here's the unreasonable part of all this: Jesus wants us to follow his lead on that narrow path. He doesn't pull any punches about it, either. Matthew records Jesus saying, "If any of you wants to be my follower, you must give up your own way, take up your cross, and follow me" (Matthew 16:24).

Not recorded is what I figure the person standing closest to Jesus might have said in response: "Whoa! Hey, now…*what*?"[4]

Were we to update what Jesus says, we could substitute "electric chair" for "cross." Because Jesus seems to be saying that one way or another, following him is going to be the death of us.

Like you, I'm still kicking and breathing on this earth. But I've had to die to my personal wants, dreams, and desires more than once as I've followed Jesus. I've had to embrace the truth that it's not all about me after all.

We all have experiences in life that help us die a little: the death of a family member, a lingering illness, the betrayal of a friend. We end up with scars from these experiences.

The scars may always be there—and that's okay. They're a testament to the fact that God brought us through those times.

Not around them or over them. Through them.

That's why I think Jesus is happy to share his physical scars with his disciples after his resurrection.[5] I'm sure he could have opted for a resurrection body with no scars, but he didn't. Those scars weren't shameful. They were badges of honor. They were evidence of his journey as Messiah.

And just like Jesus' scars show his decision to walk the narrow road, my scars and your scars are part of our journey to become who God has made us to be. To get us to where God wants to take us.

Peter Rollins, in his book *Insurrection*, writes about the *deus ex machina*. In ancient Greece, playwrights sometimes found they needed to add a dramatic turn of events in their scripts. Perhaps a character needed to die or had to settle a debt with money there was no way to obtain. So those playwrights would tie a rope to an actor and simply lower the actor into a scene to make something happen. Then the actor was winched back up off stage and out of sight.[6]

Rather than write a logical, relatable story, the playwrights dropped a god into the scene to fix the script problem.

Relying on *deus ex machina* was considered a sign of a poorly written play, by the way—and not without reason.

---

3   "Worthy Is the Lamb," Darlene Zschech, Hillsong
4   Loosely translated from Aramaic.
5   John 20:27
6   Peter Rollins, *Insurrection* (New York, Howard Books, 2011), 12.

I think we tend to treat God the same way. At least I know I do. I want out of my current job, so I beg God to just show up and change it. I don't want to deal with an illness, so I request an instant miracle.[7]

Yet when the life of faith calls me to stay on a difficult path rather than detour off onto an easier road, those are precisely the times I learn how much God cares about me. That's when I discover yet again that even when I'm needful, he sticks with me. That he wants to be with me, to comfort me, to walk with me.

To be my friend.

Because you can't find a better friend than one who won't abandon you when times get tough. Solomon says it this way: "A friend is always loyal, and a brother is born to help in time of need" (Proverbs 17:17).

You find out who your friends are when it doesn't benefit them to be around you.

This is a dynamic that frequently comes up for us runners.

When I go out for a run on my own, I run at my own pace. I have a watch to keep track of my time, and if I'm feeling great and want to run fast, that's what I do.

And on those days I feel like my shoes are lined with lead, I slow down my pace.

When I'm running alone, I set my own pace. But that changes when I'm running with a friend.

If that friend is slower than I am, I limit myself to the speed my friend can handle. And when I'm running with someone faster than I am, that friend stops and waits for me now and then along our route.

I get the best workout when I run at the optimum speed for my own body, but when I'm running with a friend, my priority changes. I stick with that friend rather than do what will give me the best workout return. Running with a slower friend limits the physical benefits, but I choose to do what's best for the relationship.[8]

My recent job transition led to a challenging season of life for me. I wondered what God's plan was. I begged for details but didn't receive any. During this time, there was a small number of friends who kept sending me encouraging cards or messages.

Those cards and messages are like jewels in my memory. These people showed me they still cared about me as a person when I was down and out. Now that I've come out of that time of uncertainty, my gratitude for those few people and their generosity is immeasurable. They gave of themselves at a time

---

7   See my comments in chapter 10 about trying to manipulate God.
8   I used to run ahead and do push-ups. Now I lag behind and try not to die. Either my friends are getting faster, or…no, that's it. There's no other possibility. NO OTHER POSSIBILITY, I SAID! (puts fingers in ears) LALALALA I CAN'T HEAR YOU LALALALA

I had nothing to give them in return. They slowed down when they could have just run ahead.

The body of Christ is designed to be a community that sticks with us when no one else will. It's all too true that we don't always get it right, but here's the good news: Next time someone is down and out, you can choose to respond differently. You can stay by that person's side.

You can take up the unreasonable expectation of Jesus that we walk the narrow, difficult road of acting in ways that may be hard but are ultimately healthier for us and for the body of Christ.

And Jesus isn't expecting anything from us that he's not willing to do himself. Consider: "God showed his great love for us by sending Christ to die for us while we were still sinners" (Romans 5:8).

Jesus is still in the business of loving us when we least deserve it, in being faithful when we are faithless. It's his love for us that causes him to stick with us even when we're struggling to stay on that narrow path. And it's this incredible, narrow-path kind of love that tells us that his calling us into relationship is born of love, not obligation.

If we take shortcuts in our faith, we miss the most important lesson of all: We don't serve an unreliable genie who occasionally grants wishes; we serve a loving God who draws closer to us when we need him most.

Because that's what happens when you're in community. That's what love does and then does again and again.

I know it can be easy to view the language of the narrow path and gate as being critical. As a way to hammer ourselves and others when we don't live up to who God has called us to be.

"Not everyone is going to get through the gate, brother; just those who pray enough. Or read the Bible enough. Or tithe." That sort of thing.

But before you jump right to the idea that Jesus is holding a ruler and looking forward to rapping you on the knuckles, I want to point out two things.

First, Paul wrote, "So now there is no condemnation for those who belong to Christ Jesus" (Romans 8:1). So Jesus isn't saying this to make you feel ashamed.

Second, Jesus invites everybody to join him on the narrow path. It's available to anyone and everyone who wants to choose it. Even imperfect people like me! And you!

So let's not pull this caution from Jesus out of a larger context: He's come to save all who are lost, all who will come stumbling toward him reaching out to him. It's not our job to convince them they'll never be good enough to squeeze into the Kingdom.

Jesus is plenty able to take all who want to go with him.

He's unreasonable like that.

Here are a few thoughts about how we might want to navigate that narrow road in our own lives:

Practice the narrow road.

You don't show up to a race hoping you can pull it off. You get ready for the race. You train. You determine what attitudes and behaviors will put you in the best possible shape to run and run well.

That's true when lacing up your track shoes to pound out a marathon and true when you're getting ready to walk a narrow path.

Among other decisions I've made that have helped me stick closer to that narrow path Jesus calls me to walk is this: I fast.[9]

I've brought up fasting before, and there's a reason for it: It is *outstanding* at getting you quickly to the next thing I suggest.

Focus on Jesus.

The easiest way to stay on the path is to follow someone ahead of you who's on it, and that's Jesus.

Pay attention to him. Pay *ridiculous* attention to him, keeping an ear cocked to hear his voice, an eye looking for how he might be leading you.

When you read something unreasonable Jesus said, including in places other than the Sermon on the Mount, lean in. Ask how you can incorporate his words into your life. Narrow-path living is going to take some counterintuitive ideas that only Jesus can help us grab hold of.

Nobody else is able to help you navigate that narrow path like Jesus.[10]

Don't try to do it alone.

The narrow road is difficult. And I don't see anywhere in Jesus' comment that you have to go it alone.

Being involved in community is crucial. You wouldn't climb Mount Everest alone. Why would you undertake a challenging spiritual journey that goes against your natural preferences and inclinations without people who will help and encourage you along the way?

And when I say "be involved in community," I don't mean you just show up at church on Sunday. By itself, that's not going to cut it.

Build friendships. Choose other people who you'll be open with about what's going right and what's going wrong in your life. Meet regularly. Talk freely. Be transparent so you can come alongside one another in meaningful, honestly supportive ways.

Use every tool at your disposal.

When you're mountain climbing, you bring tools to help you get up the mountain safely. Depending on the mountain, you could be hauling along proper shoes, chalk, oxygen, parkas, water, food, tents, ropes, or a thousand other tools that could save your life.

---

9   All this talk of fasting is making me hungry.
10 Not even this author, no matter how devastatingly handsome or gloriously bearded.

There are tools to help you stay on the narrow path, too.

You can read books that provide perspectives on living the life of faith.[11]

You can listen and participate in worship music anywhere there's a computer.

You have ubiquitous access to the Bible, God's grand narrative that points us to his ultimate purpose of restoring this broken and flawed world and invites us to be part of it.

If you're struggling with a hurt, habit, or hang-up that's too heavy to drag up the narrow path, there are support groups like Celebrate Recovery to help you handle the load. I know people who attend a support group every night of the week because they desperately don't want to make unhealthy choices.

Maybe some of your tools are about addition by subtraction.

For instance, there's software you can load on computers to prevent access to websites with unhealthy content. Or, heck, you can downgrade from a smartphone to a dumb phone if you need to. That can help for anything from an addiction to pornography to an addiction to social media.

Were I to start hiking up Mount Everest tomorrow, I wouldn't make it far before realizing I need the proper equipment, training, and support team.

The narrow road is no different.

I rejoice when anyone starts walking that narrow path, but I know they'll need help. As the church, it's our job to offer support so they don't give up before they really get started.

In the era before GPS (or, as I call it, the darkest age of humankind), if friends wanted to come over to my house, I had to give them directions. I've already mentioned I'm direction-challenged, and that extended to giving terrible directions to others if they were unfortunate enough to ask for my help.

You had, at best, a 50-50 shot of making it to my place.[12]

Had I told you that coming to my place involved driving up a steep, muddy, rocky lane with a no-guardrail, thousand-foot drop-off on one side, you'd probably rethink whether you really wanted to come visit. Was my company and the food I'd serve really worth the trouble and the risk associated with the drive?

I love how honest Jesus is with us when he's giving us directions to that narrow gate leading deeper into the Kingdom.

"It's a long, difficult journey. Most people would rather stay on the highway. The highway doesn't go anywhere worth going, but it sure is easier than navigating the turnoff to my place."

Were I Jesus' marketing manager, I'd want him to downplay that a bit.

---

11 I'd recommend any of the books you see mentioned in my footnotes throughout this book.

12 More Kung Pao chicken for me, I say.

But Jesus values us enough to be open and up front. No gimmicks. No tricks. No bait and switch. He doesn't hide the unreasonable parts of a life of faith; he puts them on display.

The beauty, of course, is that it all points to our need for the transforming power of the Holy Spirit,[13] which God also freely gives.

Thank God for an unreasonable Savior we can trust, even when he's letting us know there's a challenging road ahead.

---

13   Romans 8:11; Romans 12:2; Matthew 7:11; chapter 13

▌▌ A Brief Pause

A narrow road. A difficult road. A road not everyone who hears Jesus is willing to walk. But it's the road he's on, and—if we intend to follow him—it's the only road we can walk.

Picture Jesus' face as he's delivering this portion of his sermon. What do you see in his eyes as he speaks? What does that tell you about him?

_____

_____

_____

_____

I mentioned that I now cherish my difficult days because they made me who I am. What's an experience you hated as you walked through it, but now you see the value of having had the experience?

_____

_____

_____

What's a decision hanging out in front of you that's a "narrow path" decision? Something you think Jesus is calling you to do but you're not quite sure whether you're willing to go there yet?

_____

_____

_____

Chapter 16

THE TREE AND ITS FRUIT

*Beware of false prophets who come disguised as
harmless sheep but are really vicious wolves. You
can identify them by their fruit, that is, by the way
they act. Can you pick grapes from thornbushes,
or figs from thistles? A good tree produces good
fruit, and a bad tree produces bad fruit. A good
tree can't produce bad fruit, and a bad tree can't
produce good fruit. So every tree that does not
produce good fruit is chopped down and thrown
into the fire. Yes, just as you can identify a tree by
its fruit, so you can identify people by their actions.*

—Matthew 7:15-20

I love this part of the Sermon on the Mount.

Jesus basically says, "Talk is cheap. People will show you who they are with their actions, and you'll show others who you are by your actions."

I love it because it reminds me that being a follower of Jesus isn't about maintaining appearances.

When I was a teenager, I was once called out from the pulpit by a pastor who, in front of hundreds of people, let me know he was unhappy I'd showed up for church in jean shorts and a T-shirt. Since I didn't care about church much in those days, I wasn't worried about the public scolding. And on future occasions when I accompanied my mom to church, I kept wearing jean shorts and T-shirts.[1]

---

1   I really explored my stubbornness during the teenage years. All three of my kids are at least as stubborn as I am, and my oldest is just crossing from tween into teen. Please pray for me.

I had this idea that God wasn't concerned or offended by what I wore, but rather with whether I loved God. I continue to hold that opinion.

Now, if someone wants to dress up to honor God, that's wonderful. I have no problem with that in the least. But when someone's attire is viewed as evidence of his or her true respect and devotion to God—or lack thereof—that's when I have a problem.

A friend recently told me that when he was young, if his family's finest clothes weren't clean on Sunday morning, his family just skipped church. They knew others would look down on them.

The "fruit" Jesus talks about in this portion of his sermon is so much bigger than silly competitions about what we wear. He's talking about something deeper, something giving evidence of inner change.

And just as all believers are called to be genuinely transformed by the Holy Spirit, so much more are the pastors—the "prophets" of our day.[2]

I've had enough experiences in ministry to know there are quite a few wolves in pastors' clothing. Some want money. Some want power. And some look and sound a lot like those pastors who are serving for all the right reasons.

So how can you tell the faithful shepherds from the wolves who impersonate them? How do you know who to trust and respect?

Jesus tells us exactly how: by observing them. He's not deputizing us as "Jesus Police," calling us to confront pastors any time we disagree with something they do or say.[3] But we *are* to be looking for evidence that a pastor's faith is authentic, resulting in spiritual growth.

Paul outlines qualities that show up in our lives when we allow the Holy Spirit to transform us.[4] That's the fruit Jesus says should be in evidence in the life of not only pastors but each of us.

"Now hold on a minute," you might be thinking. "Didn't Jesus, *in this very same sermon*, tell us not to judge others? Yet here he's telling us to make determinations based on outward results. Not only does this seem unreasonable…but it looks like a double standard."

Excellent point. Let me explain why there isn't a contradiction here.

When Jesus tells us not to judge, he's talking about a very specific kind of judgment: hypocritical judgment. *That's* a double standard: applying one set of rules to our own behavior and another set to everyone else.

---

2   If you're into biblical studies and you're worried I'm confusing the office of prophet with the office of pastor, note that I'm simply seeing Jesus' reference here as being to those who are in positions of spiritual leadership. I'm not trying to blur any distinctions that are made in other portions of Scripture.

3   *Jesus Police* would also be a terrible idea for a new reality show. Like *COPS*, but just people accusing others of not being filled with the Holy Spirit. (…thinking…) You're right. Still not as bad as some of the stuff already out there.

4   I'll save you from flipping back to chapter 4. Galatians 5:22-23 says the products of the Holy Spirit in our lives are love, joy, peace, patience, goodness, kindness, gentleness, faithfulness, and self-control.

But once we have the speck out of our own eye, we can start looking for evidence of the Holy Spirit's work in ourselves and others. Not for the purpose of condemning, criticizing, or making ourselves look better, but so we can encourage others as they grow more like Jesus, as they stick on that narrow road.

Clear-eyed judging is an opportunity to build up, not tear down. And it's helpful because if we (or others) aren't seeing spiritual growth, it's time to consider new strategies in our lives.[5]

I was once part of a church plant (that is to say a brand-new church trying to get launched) in the Dallas-Fort Worth area.

The pastor asked all the leaders to join him as he visited all the households in a particular townhome community near the hotel where our church met. The goal was to invite everyone to join us at our Easter Sunday grand opening.

This particular housing area had a large number of people who spoke Spanish as their primary language, so I pulled out my rusty high school Spanish as I enthusiastically invited dozens of families to join us.

It quickly dawned on me that I couldn't remember how to say "Easter" in Spanish. As this was before the days of smartphones, I did my best to communicate using the words I could remember. I knew how to say "eggs" in Spanish (*huevos*), so I invited people to attend the *fiesta con los huevos*. I collected a few funny glances but figured I was still getting my message across.

After an hour of knocking on doors, our canvassing team touched base before heading off for the day. I asked the pastor (who was fluent in Spanish) how to say "Easter," and he told me it was *Pascua*. I'll never forget how to say "Easter" in Spanish again, and in a moment you'll understand why.

When I told the pastor I'd figured out how to communicate "Easter" without actually knowing the right word, he raised a quizzical eyebrow and asked what, exactly, I'd been saying.

I proudly recounted my ingenious approach of inviting people to "the party with the eggs." The pastor froze in his steps and turned around, wide-eyed. Wearing that grave gaze pastors usually reserve for funeral services, he quietly asked me to point out which doors I'd knocked on. I had to admit that I'd knocked on so many that I wasn't sure I could retrace my steps. He hung his head, sighing, clearly feeling defeated.

I learned that while *huevos* means "eggs" in Spanish, it's also slang for "testicles."

I'd just canvassed a neighborhood telling people that our church would be having a testicle party at the local hotel up the street in a couple of weeks and we'd not only like them to show up but also wanted them to bring their kids.

---

5   Useful tool to determine whether you're ready for clear-eyed, helpful judging: When somebody makes you aware of something unhealthy or unhelpful in your life, how do you respond? Are you defensive or open to receiving correction? The latter is a good sign you're ready to be of service to others.

You might be shocked to learn that not a single family I invited showed up at our Easter service.[6]

My point: Even though my intentions were pure and good, there's no way you could call my efforts successful, because my actions didn't bear the fruit our team was after. It's a funny story, but in a cross-cultural how-to guide, you wouldn't point to what I did as a recommended procedure.

If while looking at religious leaders—and at ourselves—we see questionable fruit sprouting, that's a sign a change is needed. Maybe it's a need to grow in our friendship with Jesus, to be more open to the Holy Spirit's nudging toward truth and holiness. Maybe there's a need to confess sin and engage more fully with the deep healing Jesus wants to bring about in our lives.

A caution: I'm *not* saying that if only good things (that is, things that make your life easier) happen, it's a sign all is well with you spiritually.

You may be honoring God and living faithfully and still have the roof cave in on your life. That adversity may be just what God knows you need to draw you even closer to him.

Unreasonable, isn't it?[7]

Pretty much everywhere else in life—at school, on the basketball court, at work—when you do good stuff, you get rewarded. So having lots of good stuff is a sign that you're doing something right. Probably a lot of things right.

But in the Kingdom Jesus describes, it's all about the heart. And one way to get a glimpse of the heart is to carefully look for the evidence of the fruit Jesus describes. A holy person and an evil person can both be wealthy, but they'll have very different ideas about how important their fortune is and how they'll use it.

In *Mere Christianity*, C. S. Lewis uses an analogy about being a disciple of Jesus that I believe helps explain what Jesus is saying here. Lewis says our lives are like a house.[8]

Before we invite Jesus into our house, it's a filthy mess, a mess we really can't do much about. The plumbing and electricity don't work properly; it's dank and moldy; the whole place is in a state of disrepair.

But when we invite Jesus in, he starts fixing the things that are broken. He starts cleaning up the place.

There are a few rooms we don't want Jesus to see, but eventually we understand he doesn't want us to have just an adequate house. No, he wants us to have a fully *restored* house—one that's as good as new.

We're ecstatic! A place that was miserable and depressing is becoming something beautiful and joyful. We're happy and thankful as Jesus' renovations and repairs allow us to enjoy living our lives in an entirely new way.

---

6   I'll give you 30 seconds to stop laughing at me. Okay. That's enough. Really. All done now.

7   Job would most likely agree. So would Joseph. And Esther. And Naomi. And David. And Jesus. You get the picture.

8   C. S. Lewis, *Mere Christianity* (New York, HarperCollins), 205.

We enjoy our new house and living in it with Jesus.

And that's when he pulls out a sledgehammer and starts knocking down a wall. Ripping off the wallpaper. Destroying the deck so he can pour concrete into a new foundation for the new extension.[9]

Jesus isn't a housekeeper; he's an architect. Not only is he not here to keep our house "clean enough," but he's here to create the house *he* has in mind. And where the new house and the old house aren't compatible, the old house has to go.

When Jesus shows up in our lives in a fresh and powerful way, fixing what's worn and broken, clearing the dirt off what we've let decay, we expect it's time to start the party. We've arrived.

But that's just the beginning. That's when the real work starts. The changes Jesus intends to make in you aren't weekend projects; they're ongoing. And like most renovations, things often get messier before they get better.

For the fruit of the Holy Spirit to sprout naturally from your life takes more than making a few cosmetic changes to your house. It requires transformation from the inside out.

That's what Jesus is urging his audience to search for in the lives of their religious leaders…and themselves.

Good fruit is evidence that the Holy Spirit is working to do more than make my disgusting house look better. It means I'm on the way to having a new house at the end of the process.

Transformation is hard to measure and easy to fake.

But if you're taking Jesus' sermon to heart, and you're willing to be honest, here are a few questions to ask yourself. Your answers will give you what my answers give me: a glimpse into how the Holy Spirit's remodeling is going in my life.

How are you different now from the way you were before you met Jesus?

I mean, seriously. If I'm listening to Jesus, things will change. The trajectory of my life will land me in a different place from where I was headed when I wasn't following Jesus.

I realized a while back (not as far back as I wish) that following Jesus isn't a process of getting him on board with what I'm doing. Rather, it's the process of me getting on board with what he's doing.

My prayers have changed from "God, bless my plans and make them successful" to "God, what are you up to and how can I get on the bus?"

Before I started following Jesus, I was the most sarcastic, egotistical jerk you could imagine. I can still be sarcastic, egotistical, and a jerk, but it's a lot less

---

9   BTW, unlike *Jesus Police*, this is a great idea for a new reality show. Guy shows up in somebody's house, gets a tour, and then breaks down a wall to start renovations with no forewarning. Call me, HGTV.

often and it's far less intense.[10] Following Jesus has changed me in a way I'd never have managed on my own.

Pausing to look backward can help you understand the trajectory God has you on and can point you toward where you're going.

What are the areas of your life in which God is transforming you?

The biblical narrative is pretty clear that we'll never be 100 percent perfect in this life.[11] So if we say, "You know, I'm good. I don't really need God's help anymore," we're not making a sound decision.

There are *always* areas of our lives in which inviting God to bring transformation to us is a good call. If you're unsure what those areas are, ask your spouse, kids, loved ones, or co-workers. Trust me, they know.

If you're not being changed by the Holy Spirit, it's time to reassess your surroundings and to chop down anything that's not bringing you into God-community. But one warning about this: Don't use this as an excuse to attack or blame other people.

Paul is very clear that in addition to there being a God who loves us and wants us in community, there's also an enemy of God's Kingdom who wants to prevent us from enjoying a healthy, life-giving community with God and one another. We're all born on a battlefield, but other people are never our true enemy.[12] Our real enemy is this adversary, this "accuser" we call Satan.

Satan may work through other people at times, but again, people are *never* our ultimate enemy.[13]

So let's not let the process of shedding those things in life that hold us back from God-community be an excuse to attack or cut off others. Earlier in his sermon, Jesus tells us to love our enemies, and it can start here.

If you feel another person or group of people are in the way of experiencing the transformation God wants to do in your life, consider doing the following: Forgive them, pray for them, and then create some healthy boundaries for how you interact with them.

In some cases, this may mean severing a relationship. But especially in cases where we're dealing with close family, that may not be an appropriate option. Besides, perhaps some of the transformation God wants to bring about in you will come through those very relationships.

Are you contributing to a healthy church culture of transformation?

Just as we as individuals can see fruit in our lives, churches can see the same. If that

---

10   Definitely at least a 1.7 percent decrease.
11   1 Timothy 1:15; Isaiah 53:6; Isaiah 64:6; and so on
12   Ephesians 6:12
13   Not even most Yankees fans. Okay, not even *all* Yankees fans.

fruit isn't evident, perhaps we might consider that our faith community would benefit from some transformation.

Because I need a healthy faith community...and you do, too.

My faith community holds up a mirror so I can see what kind of fruit is coming out of my life.

A mirror is always honest. It comes with no expectations. It's never motivated by jealousy or cruelty. We do well to make our faith communities, our churches, places of honesty. Places where "speaking the truth in love" isn't code for "permission to be a jerk." Places where the doors are truly wide open and inviting.

Which can be a challenge. Any community quickly settles into a set of expectations and norms. Even without realizing it, rules and standards emerge. A culture comes into focus, a "way we do things around here."

So when someone who doesn't fit the mold shows up, he or she might get a chilly reception.

Christianity has far too often sent the message that if you want to belong in a church community, you must behave in certain ways first.

You can't come to church if you smoke or drink or cuss or dress inappropriately or if you don't look like us or if you're a single parent or if you vote the wrong way or if you're divorced or...well, just fill in the blank.

But that's not the Gospel.

Jesus never demands that people "act properly" before they spend time with him. The message of the Gospel is that we belong before we ever behave in healthy ways, and that belonging will end up influencing how we behave.

To restate that: We aren't told to behave *before* we belong but rather that we belong right from the moment we want to belong. And that belonging is part of transforming who we are—which then affects our behavior.

If belonging to the body of Christ doesn't affect our behavior or actions, then something has gone wrong. That may be our fault, or perhaps the faith community we're part of is unhealthy, but something is wrong.

If God's heart is to draw us into community with himself and one another, then church must be a place that helps people find that sense of community.

Because once a person is in true community with God, and by the power of the Holy Spirit that person wants to follow Jesus, that's when the person begins living out the healthy practices and perspectives Jesus calls us to experience.

Horse before the cart stuff, not the other way around.

So our challenge in our own lives and the context of our faith communities: Will we be as graceful with others as God has been with us? We're grateful *we* don't have to earn God's love, blessing, or salvation with our actions—and that's great. We *should* be grateful.

But will we extend that incredible grace to others who are just starting the process of transformation? those whose fruit is just beginning to bud?

▮▮ A Brief Pause

When God-fueled transformation happens, there's evidence. It shows up in our actions. Our attitudes. Our relationship with him and others. Answer the questions below, but before you do, ask Jesus how *he'd* answer them.

How are you different now from before you met Jesus?

_____

_____

_____

_____

What are the areas of your life in which God is transforming you?

_____

_____

_____

_____

In what ways are you contributing to a healthy church culture of transformation?

_____

_____

_____

_____

Chapter 17

TRUE DISCIPLES

Not everyone who calls out to me, "Lord! Lord!" will enter the Kingdom of Heaven. Only those who actually do the will of my Father in heaven will enter. On judgment day many will say to me, "Lord! Lord! We prophesied in your name and cast out demons in your name and performed many miracles in your name." But I will reply, "I never knew you. Get away from me, you who break God's laws."

—Matthew 7:21-23

Were I ranking topics that make me internally cringe, hell is definitely way up there on the list.

In my struggle to reconcile hell with my faith in a loving God, I've done a good deal of praying. And thinking. And reading. Trust me, there's a *ton* of material written about hell.[1]

But no matter how much praying, reading, and thinking I do, I can't wash away my overall revulsion to the idea that some people will suffer in a place of fire and agony for eternity. The very idea almost makes me nauseous.

I don't want that for my worst enemy.

---

1   I'd recommend reading multiple books that embrace multiple perspectives—from *Kingdom, Grace, Judgment* by Robert Capon to *Erasing Hell* by Francis Chan. Reading multiple perspectives—even those you don't agree with—can help you develop your own understanding of theological topics. The starting point should always be reading the Scriptures for yourself, though, and inviting the Holy Spirit to give you understanding.

What's more, if I'm in the fully realized Kingdom of God—heaven—how can I have true peace when part of me is grieving for the souls suffering in hell? I can't imagine heaven as a place where it's okay to ignore or mock those in hell.

While Jesus doesn't specifically mention hell in this portion of his sermon, he refers to a judgment day and indicates that some people won't make it into heaven.

I don't think there's any question that his audience fills in the blank when considering where someone *not* getting into heaven was headed: hell.[2]

And while Jesus doesn't camp out on hell, delivering a fire and brimstone warning to those who aren't walking the straight and narrow, some of his spokespeople talk about little else.

Like you, I've encountered sidewalk preachers who warn anyone and everyone within range of their bullhorns about the torments of hell unless listeners repent and accept Jesus.

Cars and trucks painted with warnings about eternal damnation for those who aren't saved have zipped past me on the highway. I've had people knock on my front door and explain how they wanted to help me avoid a terrible fate in the afterlife.

Here's my concern with these mentions of hell: I don't see much similarity between them and how Jesus conducted his ministry.

Rather than trying to move people into relationship by hanging hell over their heads as a threat, Jesus spends most of his time talking about the Kingdom of God. Which makes sense to me. Why focus on hell when Jesus can talk instead about the full, vibrant life God wants to give to those who embrace him?

Here's a timely example: We're nearly at the end of the Sermon on the Mount and Jesus is just now getting to the topic of hell.

It's not that Jesus ducks talking about hell. He just doesn't make it the headline of his ministry. And I think we'll do well to follow his example.

Still, there it is: hell.

A topic that—at first glance—might feel entirely unreasonable. So unreasonable that the very mention of hell can cause some people to walk away from God. Because God + Love = Hell is a pretty hard equation to accept.

And since Jesus *is* God, Jesus goes in the rearview mirror, too.

But if I don't want to take that path—the one away from a life of faith—it seems I have two options for resolving my discomfort regarding hell…at least based on how the church has traditionally understood hell.

---

2 They may or may not have had in mind the same thing we think of when we hear that word, but some kind of judgment in the afterlife was commonly accepted. In Luke 16, Jesus tells the story of the rich man and Lazarus, and he incorporates afterlife imagery, which is likely indicative of common understanding at the time. The rich man is described as being "in anguish in these flames" (v. 24).

One option is I can accept there's a place of fiery torment. People who follow Jesus go to heaven, and people who don't follow Jesus go to hell, so I'd best do all I can to be on the right side of that equation and get others there as well.

Or—option number two—I can decide to dismiss hell. Decide that because it's hard for me to reconcile a loving God with eternal punishment, hell must not exist.

But since Jesus didn't dismiss hell, option two seems…risky.

It's a risk many people choose to take. They—and maybe you—hit the topic of hell, and it completely contradicts the loving God we want to worship. The forgiving Jesus we've come to know.

So we distance ourselves. We aren't sure we want to be in a relationship with someone who hands out sentences of eternal torment. Anyone who does that seems like…well, a monster, not a Messiah.

Do this for me: Don't walk away. Keep an open mind and consider the following:

God is smarter than I am…and smarter than you, too.

In *The Great Divorce*, author C. S. Lewis posits an idea: that everyone in hell can leave any time they want, but the vast majority of hell's residents choose not to do so.[3]

Essentially Lewis says that hell is a place of separation from God, and those who've lived in such a way that they landed in hell have no interest in getting closer to God. They prefer to live in a dreary wasteland of perpetual isolation. There's a bus that runs between hell and heaven, but even those who board the bus almost always return to hell. If you're interested in why, you should totally read the book.

What I like about Lewis' explanation isn't that it's necessarily correct. What I like is that I would never have thought of it. Like…never.

And if a human like Lewis can come up with a plausible explanation for why people in hell might want to stay there, I have great hope that God (who's smarter than Lewis *and* me) has a way to resolve my dilemma about hell that I can't even begin to anticipate now.

Just because I see a two-sided problem doesn't mean that God doesn't see a hundred different options I can't even consider.

Plus, Lewis' idea is something other than annihilationism or universal reconciliation,[4] both of which I find incredibly problematic.

Bottom line: If we're trying to sand the rough edges off God—concerning hell or anything else—we're way off base. God doesn't need PR spin. He also isn't going to play by whatever rule book we try to impose on him or the afterlife.

---

3   C. S. Lewis, *The Great Divorce* (New York, HarperCollins).
4   Ten dollar theological terms for $500, Alex…

God is different from me.

We've already considered (chapter 2) how God exists outside of time. The realms of heaven and hell also apparently exist in this nonphysical plane of existence.

So even if I talk about an eternity in hell, I have no idea what that actually means. For me, yesterday is past, tomorrow is future, and eternity is far beyond my understanding. And I'm absolutely clueless what "eternity" means when experienced outside the realm of time.

Spending eternity in hell may not be at all what we think it is. So hold off on judging God until you see what he's actually doing.

God is more loving than I am.

When I eventually "know everything completely" (1 Corinthians 3:12), including the nature and reality of hell, I believe I'll respond by saying, "God, you're so merciful, generous, and loving! I can't believe how great you are! I thought hell was this terrible thing, but now I see it's all part of your love and generosity!"

I may not know exactly how hell works, but I do know God isn't a mean kid on an anthill with a magnifying glass, burning people for entertainment. So whatever God is doing with the afterlife, it's loving, not hateful.

I'm not saying that because God is loving, a hell of eternal suffering is impossible. I'm saying that whatever God is doing, when we get the full picture, we'll see his actions have always been loving and we'll worship God all the more, not pull back out of fear or sadness.

Pastor Timothy Keller says that God's actions are exactly what we would do, if we knew everything he does.[5]

And that's where I place my faith: in a God who's loving, good, and generous. Again and again I've discovered that when I think God is none of those in some situation, it's because I didn't have the full picture.

I wish I had a more satisfying answer for dealing with hell than "have faith," but that's the life Jesus-followers signed up for—trusting him when we don't understand.

So when the question "What do you believe about hell?" or "How can you believe in a being that will send people to eternal torment?" arises, we can say, "What I know is that God is loving and Jesus offers us the opportunity to have the fullest possible life starting here and now."

We're not the judge. We're not the jury. Nobody will or won't go to hell on our say-so.

We're the redeemed, thankful for grace and eager for everyone to enjoy a full friendship with God through the sacrifice of Jesus, the Messiah.

---

5   Tweet from @timkellernyc on January 20, 2014

▌▌ A Brief Pause

Hell: That's the stop where lots of people step off the "I'm-interested-in-Jesus" train. Maybe it's where you exited, too. If everything Jesus does is motivated by relationship and love, how can we explain hell?

What does this portion of Jesus' sermon tell you about him? about his heart for people? for you?

_____

_____

_____

In what ways is the topic of hell challenging for you—or isn't it a challenge? What will you do to address that challenge?

_____

_____

_____

_____

For me, it took time to take my trust in God and apply it to this area. Has that been challenging for you as well?

_____

_____

_____

_____

Chapter 18
BUILDING ON A SOLID FOUNDATION

Anyone who listens to my teaching and follows it is wise, like a person who builds a house on solid rock. Though the rain comes in torrents and the floodwaters rise and the winds beat against that house, it won't collapse because it is built on bedrock. But anyone who hears my teaching and doesn't obey it is foolish, like a person who builds a house on sand. When the rains and floods come and the winds beat against that house, it will collapse with a mighty crash.

—Matthew 7:24-27

And so we come to the end of the Sermon on the Mount—what I consider to be the greatest message delivered in the history of humanity.

Jesus didn't deliver his sermon to point out how much humanity stinks.

Rather, he's offering hope to anyone who cares to connect with God and is ready to acknowledge that what they've tried thus far hasn't really worked out.

He's not here to shame us for building our houses on sand; he's come to provide a rock-solid foundation to anyone interested in moving into his neighborhood. Prime real estate we never could have purchased on our own. And Jesus not only tells us we can build there but is giving us the materials we'll need to make our dwelling place there.

Really. Consider what the Apostle John wrote: "God sent his Son into the world not to judge the world, but to save the world through him" (John 3:17).

Jesus is telling his listeners that he's come to show them a better way. They no longer have to guess and worry when it comes to their relationship with

God. Was their sacrifice pure enough? Have they done enough? Have they kept the rules well enough?

None of that was going to be a deal breaker any longer. Anyone— everyone—could please God by choosing to follow Jesus no matter what they'd done or not done in the past.

That's what we *now* know, but let's look at this situation through the eyes of one of the people standing on the hillside that day.

In the course of one sermon, Jesus has just completely changed the game. And changed it in ways that are, frankly, mind-blowing.

Love my enemy?

Don't divorce whenever I feel like it?

Talk to God like we're friends?

Were it me in that crowd, I'd need some time to process this. Maybe integrate a few of Jesus' concepts into my life on a trial basis to see how it all works out. Ease into it slowly.

And that's when Jesus throws down his final unreasonable gauntlet in this sermon: If you're not building your life on his teaching, everything you're doing will be for nothing in the long run. You're not going to get the results you want. You won't enjoy the full life he has for you.

Yet even as Jesus talks about winds, rains, and floods, I don't hear him issuing threats. Rather, he's calling everyone to safety, to the redemption and restoration he's wanted for his creation since the fall of humanity.

We no longer have to be burdened with rules and regulations that only make us feel worse when we fail to live up to them. Instead, we're free to live in the grace of trusting Jesus and knowing there's no stronger foundation on which to build our lives.

But that's a hard sell for anyone who's even a little risk averse.

If some new, big-deal stockbroker told me to put all my retirement savings into one specific company, I'd be nervous. I'd want some proof it's going to work out. I'd want to see what kind of record this guy had in picking the right stocks.

I might stand on the sidelines awhile to see if his returns beat the index where I'm currently invested.

But here comes Jesus telling everyone there's no time to waste, that they have to cash out of everything else and invest in him.

Unreasonable? Standing where that crowd stood, craning their necks to see, leaning forward so they could hear, I'm guessing it sounded *very* unreasonable.

And let's admit it: It still sounds unreasonable today.

If somebody today wants to learn more about Jesus, we don't point them toward the Sermon on the Mount. We tell them to go read John first.

Jesus, it seems, doesn't understand that he needs to take things a little slower. Get people to buy in before hitting them with the heavy stuff.

But if we accept that Jesus knows what he's doing, we see he wants people to know this isn't some new philosophy you can slap onto your existing life. It's a complete life change—and one you can't pull off on your own.

This is where community plays such a vital role. Community with God and community with other people.

To build a solid foundation of faith, we *need* other people in our lives. You've heard there's no such thing as the Christian Lone Ranger. It's true. I know. I've tried and failed.

To build a house that can weather the slashing storms of trials, we need the help of others. That's one reason *now* is the time for any follower of Jesus to strengthen and expand community—with God and with his people.

There are always storms on the horizon in this life; there's no question about that. The only question is this: Where are you building your house—and who's helping you build it?

To hear the teaching of Jesus and respond with obedience in the context of relationship—of community—that's wisdom. That's where you find solid ground.

At one point in my life, I was done with church.

It was around the time that pastor's wife told my wife to leave me. It was years before I was able to let go of my anger and frustration toward "church people." Years before I realized I was missing out by writing the whole thing off.

If that's where you are, I'd like to suggest that you do something that may be uncomfortable. I'd like to suggest you get involved in a faith community.

Showing up at a church on Sunday is great, but the involvement I'm recommending, an involvement that leads to community, requires more than just spectating. It takes moving beyond casual participation and actually giving of ourselves. It also requires that we receive what others have to offer.

And depending on the size of your faith community, a Sunday morning church service may not be the right setting for any of that to happen. Getting involved with a smaller group of people, whether it's a Bible study, a small group, or a volunteer team serving in the community is crucial.

If you love Jesus but you've walked away from church because of past hurts, or because you grew frustrated with imperfect people serving in leadership, I want to beg you to consider closing that distance between you and a faith community.

I believe that what God is doing to set this world right happens not just through individuals but through all of us serving corporately as the church.[1]

Plus, if God's redemptive power isn't "strong enough" to transform those of us who are called by his name, letting us at least get along, how can we tell others about the power of Jesus Christ?

---

1   1 Corinthians 3:16

I think of it this way: If I take my daughter to an orthodontist for braces, and that orthodontist has a mouthful of teeth that look as if they're trying to escape in opposite directions, I'm not listening to his advice about how to acquire straight teeth. He clearly doesn't know.

If we Jesus-followers spend our time sniping at one another and then try to tell others about the transforming power of God's love, who's going to listen? We clearly don't know what we're talking about.

So do what I've done when I get frustrated with the church: Stick with it. Yes, I left for a while…but I'm back.

That's what happens when you're frustrated and then begin telling God about how everybody else needs to do a better job. He tells you to get back there and be part of the solution instead of part of the problem. Following Jesus means there are a few things we're not allowed to quit. Helping the local community of believers live in unity is one of them.

Maybe you've heard this quote: "Preach the Gospel at all times; when necessary, use words."[2] I used to love this quote because I thought it got me off the hook for having to walk around telling people about Jesus—something any introvert dreads.

While my understanding of evangelism has evolved since I thought this quote was my get-out-of-witnessing card, I also now realize the quote points toward something much harder than simply verbalizing my faith.

It's far easier for me to tell everyone about the wonderful words of Jesus than to actually invite the Holy Spirit into my life to transform me. To build my life on the foundation that Jesus says is going to last.

Telling others about Jesus' sacrifice is far more pleasant than sacrificing anything—perhaps everything—in the pursuit of living out a transformed life.

Marveling at how Jesus loves his enemies and his own followers who betrayed and disowned him is infinitely easier than offering forgiveness to those who belittle or hurt me.

Yet I believe this quote is close to the heart of the Gospel. Jesus himself says it's his actions that give credibility to his words.[3]

Christianity isn't a pyramid scheme where we win if people just sign up. It's about dying to ourselves and embracing a process that, in time, transforms us into new people. Without the presence of that miracle, talk is cheap.

As a minister of the Gospel, I'm convinced that my best ministry should take place inside the four walls of my own home with my wife and children. If my best ministry happens inside a church building, I'm just putting on an

---

2   This quote is frequently attributed to Saint Francis of Assisi but seems to be at the very least heavily paraphrased. In *The Rule of 1221*, Rule 11, Francis writes, "And let them show their love by the works they do for each other, according as the Apostle says: 'let us not love in word or in tongue, but in deed and in truth'" drawing on James 2:18. (Translated by Father Paschal Robinson, 1905.)

3   John 14:11

act. Any ministry happening at church should flow out of a transformed life that's lived out daily where it matters most.

Jesus' insistence that we build our lives on him doesn't allow for any posturing. We either do or don't build our lives on him. Such an unforgiving standard. Such an unreasonable demand.

Except there's love in this insistence. Jesus doesn't want us washing out to sea when the floods come, to be buried in rubble when winds howl. He wants us safe—and with him.

It's easy to read this portion of his sermon and picture him glaring at his audience, finger wagging to shame them.

Read it instead as wisdom shared. As an invitation to build where nothing can rattle you for all eternity.

That's the Jesus who's speaking.

And if you'd like to do a "foundation check," I suggest you consider these ideas:

Learn how other believers build their faith on the solid foundation.

I hear lots of churches say they "teach the Bible," and that's wonderful. Basing teaching on the Bible is an excellent idea for a church.

However, I'd still say that no church "teaches the Bible."

We all teach our interpretation, our understanding of what the Bible says. Pick any theological topic, and I can find 10 different pastors with 10 different opinions, each insisting he or she is teaching the Bible.

I say this not to dishearten you. I'm pretty sure this is according to God's design. He *wants* us to have conversations. God *wants* us to explore mysteries. God didn't have to speak through visions, songs, poems, stories, and prophecies, but he chose to do so. God could have delivered a technical manual clarifying everything, leaving nothing to interpretation, a reference guide thick with footnotes that covered every possible situation.

But he didn't.

We're simply not going to have all the answers about a life of faith in this lifetime. Not without living that lifetime by faith.

To paraphrase Søren Kierkegaard, life is "lived forward, but understood backwards."[4]

Kierkegaard's comment echoes what the Apostle Paul writes: "All that I know now is partial and incomplete, but then [in the reality of eternity] I will know everything completely, just as God now knows me completely" (1 Corinthians 13:12).

---

4   The actual quote is translated by Peter Rohde as "It is quite true what Philosophy says: that Life must be understood backwards. But that makes one forget the other saying: that it must be lived—forwards" in *The Diary of Soren Kierkegaard* (New York, Kensington Publishing Group, 1960), 111.

As I entered my seminary education, I thought I'd find answers to my questions about God and theology. I did gain some answers, but I gathered far more questions along the way—and that's okay. I can now have much better conversations about God because I have a much better grasp on the limitations of my own understanding.

When I read books or articles or blogs about topics of faith, I have the chance to see through the eyes of another person who's filled with God's Spirit. Some of those books are great conversation-starters for me and God.

Which leads me to not only better appreciate God but also better appreciate my brothers and sisters in faith.

And I've discovered this: Faith is at least as much art as science.

If you're looking to nail down satisfying answers to every question you might have about God and theology, here's something you should know: It's not going to happen.

Faith isn't something you can dissect and analyze until you completely understand it. Instead, it's something you *live*, counting on God to work in and through you.

And part of how he can equip you to faithfully follow Jesus is through exploring the perspectives of other believers.

I used to have a three-hour commute every day on a train. I'd spend that time playing games and apps or sleeping to avoid being bored.

My life was literally changed when I decided to invest those hours rather than squander them. Over the course of a year, I read dozens of books that helped open me up to new ways of thinking about Jesus, and my faith grew as a result.

You may not have time to read *dozens* of books, but I'm glad you made time to read this one. And I hope it's drawing you closer to Jesus.

If you want a foundation to stay strong, you need to do maintenance, to feed your faith—and being exposed to the thinking and encouragement of other believers is one good way to do that.

As Jesus said, when we seek something, we'll find it.[5]

Share the foundations of your faith with others.

Church is a great place for this. I sometimes hear people talk about going to church each week to "get filled up."

I respectfully think that's not a healthy way to engage in church. It sounds as if those people are just consumers.

But you and I are *not* just faith consumers. We're a canvas, one upon which Jesus is creating a masterpiece.[6] We need to share what Jesus is doing in and through us to enrich our brothers and sisters in faith.

---

5   Matthew 7:7; part of chapter 13
6   Philippians 1:6; Hebrews 12:2

Paul uses the picture of a body to describe the community of Jesus-followers.[7] It's where we get the term "body of Christ."

If you show up in your faith community to simply receive or just observe, or you're not showing up at all, we're less than whole. I need you just as much as you need me. The sooner we recognize that, the faster we can create an environment that helps us grow our faith. An environment in which we can all follow Jesus as he delivers one unreasonable challenge after another.

Because following Jesus can be hard.

Having faith when nothing makes sense and you can't catch a break is difficult.

I wish there were an easier way. I wish there were shortcuts and faith hacks that made all this a snap, but Jesus' unreasonable challenges are actually the only option open to us if we're serious about following him.

Only a group of people willing to go all in can experience the new, better life Jesus offers. Can carry out the purposes he's given us. Can build on that firm foundation he is in a shaky world.

Only when we're willing to put others before ourselves and invest in our friendship with God, will we see spiritual growth.

Either we join Jesus in being unreasonable or we miss out on what he has for us in life. Half measures don't do it, either for us as individuals or us as a faith community.

With the final words in this sermon, Jesus asks the people on that hillside and all the rest of us who've long listened in: Are you ready to get unreasonable? Because that's the only way anything will change in our lives.

As for me, I'm tired of the tyranny of reasonable expectations that crowd my life. I want to be part of something better, something bigger, something that lasts.

That's why I showed back up in church after I was completely done with it for a while.

I'm ready to embrace what will make a true difference in my life and in the lives of those around me. Something that's not going to collapse when the winds of life come howling at my door.

I'm ready to follow this unreasonable Jesus.

You in, too?

---

7   1 Corinthians 12:12-27

▌▌ A Brief Pause

Jesus wasn't content with delivering a sermon that was greeted with applause. He wanted more. He wanted obedience, for people to do what he tells us to do. That's the only way we'll have a solid foundation in life.

What's Jesus saying about himself here? about you? How do you feel about that?

_____

_____

_____

_____

_____

Let's bring this plane in for a landing. You've just heard Jesus say all sorts of unreasonable things, make all kinds of unreasonable demands of his followers. What's your response? Are you more or less hopeful? more or less excited about following Jesus?

_____

_____

_____

_____

_____

CONCLUSION

When Jesus had finished saying these things,
the crowds were amazed at his teaching,
for he taught with real authority—quite
unlike their teachers of religious law.

—*Matthew 7:28-29*

This morning, I drove my daughter into downtown Baltimore for
a doctor's appointment at Kennedy Krieger Institute, an organization that
specializes in autism-related disorders.

During my drive, somebody cut me off in an intersection and I got mad
at him. This, after writing 18 chapters about making faith practical and loving
people as Jesus loved them.

So I took a moment and prayed, "God, please fill me with your Holy Spirit.
Transform me. Help me love people, especially the inconsiderate ones."

The words of Jesus always point toward transformation. While we can take
the words of his Sermon on the Mount and distill them into practical steps,
we'll still be unable to make those changes in our lives under our own power.
We *must* allow the Holy Spirit to function in and through us to experience the
healthier life Jesus describes in his sermon.

My failures remind me of my need for a Savior. My failures also point
to God's great love, patience, and mercy.

As you seek to follow in the steps of Jesus, give yourself grace when you
fail—the same grace God offers you. Turn to God, accept his forgiveness and
grace, and ask the Holy Spirit to continue the work of transforming you into
the man or woman God created you to be.

We're all works in progress, clay pots never fully off the potter's wheel.

And Jesus is never quite done doing his work in us.

Recently, a number of billionaires pledged to give away huge portions
of their wealth to charitable causes.

Maybe you, like I do, sometimes daydream what it would be like to be
as fabulously wealthy as those billionaires. But they're not daydreaming;

they've achieved that reality. And they're giving away more money than you or I will ever cross paths with in a lifetime.

It's a shocking commitment on their behalf and, in my opinion, one that's quite commendable. Rather than reveling in the influence and power that money could buy, they're giving it away.

In the Sermon on the Mount, the living God stands in the flesh of humanity, and rather than reveling in his power over the crowds, he instead gives away the keys to having a healthy, full, abundant, eternal life.

And rather than promising secrets to attaining that life and then slowly teasing out those secrets over time, Jesus spills the beans.

In the same way that we might be utterly shocked by a politician who was completely transparent and honest, the crowds listening to Jesus were shocked to meet a famous, powerful rabbi who didn't seem to be interested in any kind of personal gain or in winning approval. Jesus didn't pander or equivocate; he laid out one challenge after another without any hint of compromise.

The things Jesus said were, frankly, unreasonable.

Yet when he spoke, I believe anyone who truly listened was strangely excited about the possibilities. They heard his words, caught his vision, but what were they supposed to do? How could what Jesus said actually come to be real in their lives?

Little did Jesus' audience know that, in a short time, the words of Jesus would be possible because of the Holy Spirit transforming lives from the inside out.

The Sermon on the Mount is the answer to that "What are we supposed to do?" question. As we let the implications of Jesus' sermon sink into us, those "whats" come into sharper focus.

The Holy Spirit is the answer to the "how" question: How are we supposed to pull this off? Given that Jesus set before us something far too difficult for us to accomplish, how do we get there?

And the answer is this: We don't. Not by ourselves.

We do it with God and with one another. And we do it not by gutting it out under our own steam but through the transforming power of the Holy Spirit.

That's the journey we're on.

It's my prayer that as together we've reflected on these words of Jesus, you've been challenged and inspired.

And it's my hope that, as you accept that Jesus was not only unreasonable but completely serious about what he said, you're inspired to pray.

Pray that God would fill your heart with the Holy Spirit so you can see continued transformation in your life and that, through us, God's Holy Spirit would renew the face of this world.

Personal Thanks:

It would be impossible for me to thank, by name, each person who has encouraged and supported me in my writing efforts. However, I am very grateful to everyone who has done so.

I'm incredibly thankful for all the people at Group Publishing who decided I had written something worth publishing and then helped me refine it into the best book it could possibly become. Foremost among them, my editor, Mikal Keefer. Simply put, this book would not exist without the support and encouragement Mikal sent my way.

This book was written during a particularly challenging season of my life, and in the midst of it, I was reminded at many turns what the body of Christ is supposed to be: a community of people who genuinely care about others.

In addition to Mikal and everyone at Group, others who have been relational and generous toward me (speaking especially of the professional realm) include Kevin Marks at Passion Publishing, George Penk at LIFE FM, Jon Seidl at The Courage, Nate Ransil at Sandy Cove, and both Sammy Foster and Steve Healy of Lighthouse Church.

My interactions with each of these people gave me more dignity than I started with. My goal is to pay that forward in every way I can.

I also wish to mention the following people who were willing to invest their time and energy into this project: Kristin Whitmore and Dottie Christianson, as well as the members of a writers collaborative I'm involved with: Luke "Gold Star" Solomon, Emily "Don't Mess With Emily" Robinson, Nick "Sigils" Anderson, and Luke "Luke" Katafiasz.

Beyond this project, I'm also grateful to have three amazing kids who let me play the role of Daddy: Naomi, Elle, and Quinn. They are the best bunch of kids any dad could have the joy to know.

And last, but certainly not least, I am deeply grateful to my wife, Liz. Your support and input has been immeasurably valuable to me in the process of writing this book. Thanks for believing in me, even when I wasn't so sure about myself.